MW00881790

Growing Up in The Big House

Alfred Spevak

Order this book online at www.trafford.com
or email orders@trafford.com

Most Trafford titles are also available at major online book retailers.

© Copyright 2015 Alfred Spevak.
All rights reserved. No part of this publication may be reproduced, stored in a retrieval
system, or transmitted, in any form or by any means, electronic, mechanical, photocopying,
recording, or otherwise, without the written prior permission of the author.

Print information available on the last page.

ISBN: 978-1-4907-5891-6 (sc)
ISBN: 978-1-4907-5893-0 (hc)
ISBN: 978-1-4907-5892-3 (e)

Library of Congress Control Number: 2015906161

Because of the dynamic nature of the Internet, any web addresses or links contained in
this book may have changed since publication and may no longer be valid. The views
expressed in this work are solely those of the author and do not necessarily reflect the
views of the publisher, and the publisher hereby disclaims any responsibility for them.

Any people depicted in stock imagery provided by Thinkstock are models,
and such images are being used for illustrative purposes only.
Certain stock imagery © Thinkstock.

Trafford rev.   04/27/2015

 www.trafford.com

North America & international
toll-free: 1 888 232 4444 (USA & Canada)
fax: 812 355 4082

Contents

MY AUTOBIOGRAPHY

by Alfred Spevak 3/16/2015A

I HAVE BEEN PLANNING ON writing this autobiography for quite some time to leave information on the events that happened during my life, for later generation's inquiry. So these are events that I remember and events that I have learned. I Wished that I had asked questions and received answers for the thoughts on my mind now. This document is not exactly in chronological order.

MY BIRTH

The Teuchert & Spevak Home early 1920's
Hilda & Alva Spevak.

I WAS THE 5TH CHILD born of Rosa and E Charles Spevak born at home in Milmont Park, Pa at my grandparent's home John & Theresa Teuchert at the corner of Milmont & Belmont Avenues numbered 131 Milmont Ave. It was a cold day of January the 16 day year of 1923 at 8AM. I was given the name of Alfred Victor Spevak. I had learned that my brother Harry 10yrs at this time with three sisters named Hilda 15yrs, Bertha 7yrs and Alva 5yrs was wishing for a brother. He was met by a friend on his way home from school that I was born. He then ran the rest of the way. I was baptized a catholic at Our Lady Of Peace Parish of Milmont Park Pa. My aunt Katherine & uncle Frank Teuchert were my god parents.

MEDICAL CARE

ABOUT THE TIME OF MY birth I became was very ill with a chest congestion and my mother Rosa and Grandmother Theresa wouldn't lie me down they kept me upright, they were afraid that I wouldn't survive. This was long before antibiotics. When you were very ill in bed as I remember the doctor was called to your home. He arrived with his satchel of pills and testing equipment. The medicines that he left were terrible tasting and my mother tried everything even money for me to take it. For a fever, the Dr Left this medication called Niter, mom would put several drops in a glass of water for me to drink. This was terrible tasting but, this was how I ended up with some cash by the time that I became well.

When you where ill you went to see your doctor at his office that was part of his residence. I remember our family Dr Clark B Stull of Ridley Park, Pa He had this stone edition built as his office an examination room attached to his home. He has scheduled visiting hours no appointment's were necessary, you just waited for your turn.

After entering his examining room and you told about your not feeling well, this initial thing happened. He put a wooden tongue depressor into your mouth and on your tongue and told to say AH to check your throat. Then he would check your ears. He checked your blood pressure and heart. Our Physician had one of those standing fluoroscope's in his office to view your chest and A short time latter it was removed, do to excessive radiation. All during the time it took to view a patient's chest the x-ray was on.

Boils were common in my early life caused by a staff infection. At times they never came to head to drain. These were very painful and this required surgery to drain.I had this done. Almost unheard of today. Many people developed appendicitis an infection and this was serious requiring a hospital stay and surgery. All of these infections just about disappeared when antibiotics came about. When I was about 16years during a winter night a group decided to go sledding on this roadway named Bullens Lane. I sledded down and was walking back up for another ride down when a another sledder coming down running into me injuring my right shin. The wound was severe and my friends pulled me home on my sled. It was late evening, our doctor was called and he said (come right over to my office). My future brother-in-law Norman Draper happening to be dating my sister Alva at this time and he drove me to Dr Stull's office in Ridley Park Pa. He cleaned my wound and applied stitches in his office. Today you would proceed to a hospital. During those times a Doctor referred you to the hospital. Back then protective gloves were only used during hospital surgery.

DENTAL CARE

DENTAL CARE. IT WASN'T VERY pleasant to have dental care In my early years, Dentist had the old fashioned drilling equipment and it was a slow process at that time. No pain killer was administered during drilling. If you had deep cavities the pain was unbearable. Not many people received preventive dental care and visited the dentists only when they had toothache. By this time the tooth was to far gone and required an extraction. They did use nova cane to eliminate pain during an extraction. During the 1930's people had teeth removed and were put under with a drug called Sweet Air which was Nitrous Oxide. This was later banned for dentistry because many people never regained conscious and didn't survived. There were no Anesthetists in those days to administer a gas or drug. This came latter. Doctors and Dentists used there own discretion at that time.

MEDICAL INSURANCE

THERE WAS NO MEDICAL INSURANCE that I know of at this time. I remember In1938 when I attained the age of 15yrs and my father E Charles arrived home from his work one evening from the Baldwin Locomotive Works with news about a new medical plan and for a monthly premium of $2.oo his family would be covered for all hospital expenses. This plan was written by Blue Cross of Philadelphia and it was non profit at this time. This plan didn't cover any doctor expenses this came later with a plan called Blue Shield that did cover surgeons and doctor expenses while hospital confined.

CATHERINE ELEANOR'S BIRTH

IN MARCH 25 1925 A sister named Catherine Eleanor Spevak was born and was given a nickname (Kitty).I being only 2 yrs at this time I was unable to remember anything about Catherine's birth, but my sister Alva Spevak Draper7 yrs at this time remembered. Alva told me not very long ago before her death, that baby Catherine developed swelling glands in her neck area and the doctor after his treatments without any improvement said to my parents that he should operate and open these glands to drain. Alva told me Baby Catherine let out a loud scream as this operation was performed on our dining room table. An infection set in and baby Catherine died in December 10 1925 after only 10 months of age. Alva said everyone cried including the doctor. Many years later, my mother Rosa, would shed tears at the mention of my sister Catherine. My father took an 8x10 portrait of Catherine when her casket was opened in our home for the viewing. I remember viewing this photo in later years as I became older. Baptized a Catholic she was buried in a Catholic cemetery.

IMMACULATE HEART OF MARY CEMETERY

MY PARENTS E CHARLES AND Rosa bought a lot just beyond the Main entrance of Immaculate Heart of Mary Cemetery in Linwood. Pa at the intersection of Laughead Ave & Market St in Linwood, Pa where Catherine was put to rest, and later with her parents E Charles & Rosa, brother Harry & his wife Estelle Spevak and their children son Paul and daughter Catherine Anne in following years. Being that I was almost 3yrs when Catherine died, I was told later that I stopped eating for a time. I always wondered that Catherine's death may have had an effect on my life. She would have been the link between Aileen and I. I always wondered how life would have been had she lived a normal life. I was told that I started talking when I was 4yrs and I really never was a big talker. I had always been a good listener and believe me I learned many things by listening. I remember many trips to this cemetery in Dad's Stearns Knight automobile touring car going down to Linwood Pa. The trip to Immaculate Heart of Mary Cemetery at that time, was passing through the city of Chester traveling west on 9th street, through Trainer Boro where the road changed name from 9th street to Ridge Rd at that time the road ran past those old mill homes in Trainer that people today had given them a nick name that isn't very nice. At a later time the road was reconstructed straight. The air in the Linwood area had a bad odor from manufacturing. Who was the contributor for this condition? well there were 3 manufacturing companies, Sun Oil, Congoleum, and American Viscose.

I read that during the Flu epidemic of 1918 relatives of people in living in Marcus Hook area came to stay, with them because the people living here weren't infected with the flu. Probably it may have been what was in the air. I was told by my parents that some people who were infected dropped dead in the street then turned black. I was told that a wagon came by to pick up the deceased, daily. The roads in the cemetery were only about 2 deep at this time and they weren't paved just cindered. I remember, where the Dairy King now stands was a business selling grave monuments. I remember some larger grave lots had fancy railings around their perimeters, these were later removed probably for easier grass cutting. It appeared that all Catholics buried from Our Lady of Peace Church in Milmont Park were buried here in Immaculate Heart Cemetery or Holy Cross Cemetery in Yeadon, Delaware County Pa.. The St Peter & Paul cemetery in Springfield was not in operation at this time.The steep grades of the roads of Yates Ave, Summit Ave and Market street leading down to Ridge Rd were paved with concrete probably to prevent washouts during heavy rain.

AMERICA'S PASTIME BASEBALL

WHEN MY FATHER E CHARLES Spevak emigrated to the United States and settled in Philadelphia he resided at 1241 Buttonwood St with his uncle Karl according to the ship SS Phoenica's manifest. This Uncle Karl was probably from his mother's side because E. Charles had a 2yr old brother named Karl when he left home for the United States in 1901.He lived close to the Phillies Ballpark, called Baker Bowl and he must have seen games played there. The American league formed about 1900 and the Philadelphia's team the Athletics was formed. There ball park called Shibe Park then later called Connie Mack Stadium was built later at 21St & lehigh Ave. When I became older my father E Charles took me there to see the A's play. In 1937 fire erupted at Baker Bowl ball park and the Phillies then moved and played their games at the Philadephia A,s park called Connie Mack Stadium. There was always a game being played at Connie Mack Stadium by one team being on the road and one home. When E Charles was a resident of the town of Stieredorf, Romania in eastern Europe, he presumably never had seen baseball being played. He became very interested in baseball. After arriving in Milmont Park in about 1918 he organized a baseball team and was the manager, it was named Forrest A C and their games were played at their home field at the intersection of Belmont & Baltimore Aves where homes stand today. I was told many people attended because of the street car. My uncle Frank Teuchert was one of the pitchers and I heard that he was very good. After final construction of MacDade Blvd in 1931, the ball field was moved to a new location along MacDade Blvd and the team changed its name to Milmont AC. Today 2012 the ball field is smaller in size and named I Walter Knoll Field a pastor emeritus of Our Lady of Peace Church. I remember in the mid 1930 watching Milmont AC playing games during Sunday afternoons. On week nights. Twilight Games were only 7 innings long. Sunday afternoon games did play 9 innings. My brother-in-law Bernard Maguire a left handed right fielder and a great batter, could really hit the long ball, many times a home run. At that time Milmont AC belonged to The Delco Baseball League.

THE TEUCHERT HOME

I LIVED IN A HOME of my grandparents.where Milk and bread were delivered each morning. A wagon from Supplee Wills Jones operated by my brother-in-law Bernard Maguire pulled by 2 horses delivered the milk and a wagon pulled by one horse pulled a Friehofers bread wagon that delivered their french loaf that was a golden brown, very delicious. Everyone liked the ends of this loaf.My grandfather John Teuchert had a new hot water heating system installed in his home during my infancy. This heated all rooms including the 3rd story. This happened about the time of my birth. I was told that it replaced an old hot air system. As I became older I became curious about this old hot air heating system and decided to investagate where I found the only heating register was in the dinning room. I assume that the only heated room was the dinning room and kitchen was heated by the coal stove. There were doors between the dining room and existing rooms. A coal fired stove in the kitchen or a fireplace in the parlor where I never saw it fired until during hurricane HAZEL in 1953 when they lost part of the power do to the storm and had no central heating. I was called and after arriving there and saw a fire burning in the fire place for the first and last time. I was able to restore electricity to have heat again.We had another room that we called (the sitting) room you would call family room by today's standards that contained our radio, piano, record player and later television.Television was a new venture after radio this new to all. They're were not programs televised until about 6pm when the local news was on and programs of entertainment started one of the first telecast was the Milton Berle's Texaco Star Theatre on NBC. Then there were the Friday Night

Fights on TV etc. These first floor rooms were separated from other unheated rooms with doors. Being that our family resided with my grandparents John & TheresaTeuchert which was to be temporary my parents Rosa and E Charles resided there many years raised there children there until the home was sold after John Teuchert's death in 1960.When John Teuchert returned home after working at The Baldwin Locomotive Works in Eddystone he remained home until the following day. My father E Charles Spevak also worked at the Baldwin Locomotive Works. My dad had other business and activities. and was out many evenings. I vaguely remember John taking me to Chester Pa on the PRT rte 76 street cars that ran past our home. He bought me some small tools, a screwdriver and a little saw etc. There were doors between the dinning room and adjacent rooms.These 2 doors were closed during the heating season when the dinning was being heated with the old hot air system. I put the screwdriver to use and started to remove the screws from the door knobs etc, I believe the screw driver was taken from me until I became a little older. Later these doors were removed after the new hot water heating system was installed and stored in the 3rd floor attic; Where my Mom Rosa Spevak would carry up her wet laundry basket up two flights of stairs to dry in the 3rd floor attic on rainy days. Rosa never complained about carrying these heavy wet baskets of clothing to dry. Other things were also stored there also, I remember a large trunk, I believe a steamer trunk that contained old clothing and remnants of christmas decorations. Our cellar was unsuitable for hanging clothes to dry. It was dusty from coal etc and had a unpaved floor.Things stored in the cellar were canned vegetables that were put up by Rosa and Theresa. Pop Teuchert also had a storage locker for his beverage of home brew and shelves for his pickled peppers My mother Rosa was always busy cooking, doing the laundry or cleaning. I remember the day that my mom and grandmom decided to white wash the basement walls. There was no need for them to do this job. One time I remember them saving the fat from cooking, then buying a can of lye (caustics) and making soap. I thought they didn't have to make soap as they had so many other things to do. Many times when you had a problem grand mom took care of it for you as Rosa my mother was busy with house work and cooking. Grandmom Theresa Teuchert took care of your cuts and bruises. Grand mom Theresa Teuchert was loved by all. When she attended the movies and took one of her grandchildren with her to Chester Pa for a day out. If you were the lucky one to go with her, it was a stop at Silver's 5&10 located at 5⁵ & Market St now called (Avenue of the states) to the refreshment bar where a large barrel of Hires Root Beer was displayed. A root beer and a hot dog sandwich really hit the spot for us young children. Then it was time to enter a movie theater, probably The Washington Theater which was close by and Where Washington House Restaurant once was next to it, a historical marker is now located where George Washington stopped by on his trip to Philadelphia Pa. Grand mom loved those romantic films with her favorite actor Rudolf Valentino. Her movie choices were not for me. I usually fell asleep. There were other movie theaters to called Stanley, State, Boyd and the Mac located further away and as us children became older we attended them. At a later date a movie opened in Eddystone called EDDY. The woman from Milmont Park went there as dinnerware was given out one piece each week. Grandmom Theresa Teuchert was A great person and she loved everyone. and was loved by everyone. One time my grandfather John Teuchert on Saturday took a trip to Chester by himself and was late getting home. He was asked about his lateness? He said (I went past the new Boyd Theater and they were celebrating their first anniversary and decided to attend a movie). This was back at about 1935 and he enjoyed it. This may have been his first movie since the silent movies that he attended. Movies had sound included in 1928. At this time the movie studios were looking for people with a nice voice and they were found the play makers on stage. The following weeks John and wife Theresa went to the movies together regularly.

15

THERESA TEUCHERT'S DEATH 1953 at 79yrs

I STILL REMEMBER THE TIME of her passing. 12/12/1953. I was married then and at 30yrs old, living in Norwood with my wife Lillian and children Alfred, Jessica, Michael and my mother in law Edna Johnson.I was called about her passing and was able to get to her home before her body was removed from her home. I understand she just was getting ready for bed when a heart attack occurred. She was 79yrs.This was a very sad day for all of us. Theresa a devout catholic attended mass daily. She is buried in Immaculate Heart of Mary Cemetery and later husband John in 1960 & son Engelbert Teuchert in 1990 and his wife Eleanor.

AILEEN MIRIAM'S BIRTH

IN OCT 14 1926 A sister named Aileen was born. I was almost 4yrs at this time. I remember Aileen at a very young age, sitting in a high chair between the kitchen stairs and the only kitchen cabinet our kitchen had and was available at this time. Aileen would eat her food and when she was finished turned the bowl over and place it on her head. She did this repeatedly. Aileen did have a beautifully head of curly hair as a child and during her life. I wonder if this had any effect? Aileen was double jointed at the first joint of her fingers, she could bend them at 90 degrees.I never saw anyone other then her being able to do this but I could wiggle my ears. As a young child I remember the white iron crib that I slept in that was located in my parents bedroom, I would wake up from a wet bed remove my wet clothing, and craw into my parents bed next to my mother and felt the comfort of mom. This bedroom was on the west side of the Teuchert home and was coolest without a closet. There was a clothes tree in on corner with a large bureau.

BREAKFAST WITH MY GRANDFATHER
JOHN TEUCHERT

AS I GOT A LITTLE older I would awake to the odor of cooking, coming up the back staircase that led into the kitchen; Grand pop John Teuchert an early riser, cooking his breakfast usually an omelet of peppers and eggs or sometimes an omelet of onions and eggs, I would go down to the kitchen and have breakfast with him, with the warmth from the coal stove it was very comfortable. Grandpa Teuchert was an early riser about 5AM and he retired in the early evening after the 7:00 PM radio news. I don't know when he slept because anything that happened during the night he knew about it. Yes we still used coal fire in our kitchen all year round to heat our domestic hot water and cooking, This caused heat to be unbearable during the summer months. At a later date a bucket a day heater was installed right below in the cellar for the hot summer months to heat our hot water. This removed the heat from a hot stove in the kitchen during the warm summer months. Many years later when I was grown I installed a gas water heater in the basement. Grandpop Teuchert prepared and bottled the beer in the basement and I remember helping him I remember going along with grand pop to a Hardware Store located at 8th & Morton Ave in Chester to buy his supplies of hops and malt for the beer making. There was a 2 burner gas range in the basement. I was with him during the beer brewing process and bottling. Pop Teuchert used these stoneware crocks for brewing. When is was ready for bottling a siphon hose was used to fill the bottles and a little funnel attachment filled with sugar and a plunger, pushed just once to insert the right amount of sugar into each bottle before capping. I liked capping the bottles. I had many memories of doing things with Pop Teuchert. He was always doing something to his home. As I got older I helped him paint the outside of his home. My grandfather purchased a new 40ft extension ladder and I being about 16 years at this time I was able to put it up by myself by putting the foot of the ladder against the house foundation to stand it up then pulling on the rope to extend it. Grand pop mixed his own paint. I remember him taking white lead, linseed oil, turpentine and Japan Drier to make the white paint and for color of gray he put a little of lamp back into it. He cut back on the amount of dryer; his paint took longer to dry. He said by limiting the amt of dryer it would last longer not flake off. One time he mixed and painted the front porch floor. It never dried. My mother Rosa and grandmother Theresa went down on their knees to scrub it clean. They gave grand pop an order to buy paint already mixed for the floor as he did after the order from his wife Theresa. We had a chain operated Coo Coo Clock on our kitchen wall just above the kitchen table. Just about everyone liked to see the coo coo come out at the hour. Grandpop occasionally would take it down to fix and oil it.

HARRY TEUCHERT'S RESCUE

I WAS ALWAYS LOOKING FOR things to make or repair. This day I was repairing an item on our kitchen table. One time a 115 volt cigarette lighter. It resembled a miniature radio speaker. I had the electric cord separated from the device. My cousin Harry Teuchert being no older than five years at ths time was sitting on top of the table. Me being so engaged in my work not paying any attention to young Harry's safety. I did hear some noise from Harry and found that he plugged the loose cord into the receptacle on the wall just above the table and grabbed the other end with just the one hand. I did come his rescue and removed the plug. His hand did have some swelling. Harry got his first electric shock.

THE CONSTRUCTION OF MACDADE BLVD

ON ABOUT 1930 A NEW road was being constructed from Chester to Darby borough. The road cut right through Ridley Township and the towns of Woodlyn, Milmont Park, Folsom and Holmes. This new road made the Ridley Township towns more accessible. I remember the old construction equipment used during this time it must had been a transition period from steam to gasoline operated equipment both types were being used. Some buildings were in its path and had to be raised or moved. The Frank Teuchert home on Virginia Ave was moved and relocated about 100 feet onto a new lot and foundation.

The Teuchert ended up with a great new location on the new road. This gave the Teuchert's great frontage along MacDade Blvd. The Teuchert's raised flowers Gladiolas and Dahlias in the field and later became florists and my Aunt Katherine made floral baskets, corsages floral deaigns for funerals.Uncle Frank built a greenhouse and showroom was built later between the garage and greenhouse and opened a business called TEUCHERT FLOWERS. My brother Harry Spevak installed a service for the garage and greenhouse. The flower shop remained until 1957, the property was sold and demolished for a Getty filling station. Which recently was demolished abt 2013 and now contains a new business called Swiss Farms. Macdade Blvd contained only two lanes at this time, one for each direction. There were no paved shoulders. You didn't drive on to the shoulders in rainy weather. You could get stuck in the mud. This was later corrected with paving. The depression had just started and probably no additional funds available for paved shoulders, they were paved later.

INSTALLING OIL HEAT IN THE TEUCHERT HOME ABOUT 1931

WHEN I WAS ABOUT EIGHT yrs of age my grandfather had oil heat installed in his home by my father E Charles and they were installing the combustion chamber with fire brick. They done this by reaching and placing the brick through the heater door opening. They came to a point where there arms could reach and go no further. How would they proceed? A plan was conceived. We will call on young AL

I WAS CALLED UPON

I WAS CALLED UPON AND they explained to me what was to be done. A little stool was placed in the heater for me to sit on. I was then shoved through the door opening and sat down on this stool as fire bricks were handed to me for placement in position. Well I felt a better when the job was done and I was able to get out, I guess claustrophobia was setting in. My brother Harry mounted an completed wiring all of the electrical equipment that was required. A small portion of the dirt floor 8in deep was removed prior where the oil tank was placed. I always thought that it would be paved with concrete There was always talk about paving the basement floor. but this never happened. This new method of heating our home was great, no more coal or ashes to shovel. We were one of the first in Milmont Park to have oil heat at this time. There were no oil dealers nearby; oil came from a dealer in Upper Darby, I still remember the name KUNKEL FUEL CO.I recall the price starting at 4 cents per gallon. When the burner was operating you could hear a ringing in the radiators. Well in later years my brother Harry was dating Estelle Bufano who later became his wife and sitting in our parlor she said to Harry she felt chilly. Harry went over to the thermostat and set it warmer.

Grandpop never missed anything, his bedroom was on the third floor and he heard the ringing in the radiator for a longer period then usual and decided to investigate. He made the trek down two flights of stairs to the living room, set the thermostat back to the normal 68 degrees. Grandpop made a remark by saying (shit)

FISHING TRIP TO CAPE MAY AND CRABBING IN DELAWARE

GRAND POP TEUCHERT DIDN'T CARE for sports unless it was deep sea fishing, until a TV was bought and installed by his daughter Millie Teuchert Ingram. We would be watching baseball and Pop Teuchert got interested and kept asking us about the game. My grandfather never drove and many times employees that worked with him at the Baldwin Locomotive Works would stop by and pick him up for a fishing trip to Delaware or New Jersey that he loved to do. When I was about 8 yrs, POP Teuchert decided to take me on a fishing trip to Cape May NJ. This was my first fishing trip on a charter boat. Pop had this bright green fishing basket with his rod and reel. Being that pop didn't drive we used public transportation. We boarded the # 76 street car at Belmont & Milmont Ave's on its arrival from Chester to its destination Darby. Where we boarded another street car for Philadelphia's waterfront, where we boarded the ferry to Camden NJ and boarded a Reading Railroad train for Cape May NJ and when we reached Cape May we boarded a fishing boat. I remember it was a bright warn sunny day. The boat proceeded quite a distance out of sight from land. A crew member tossed a line overboard with an attachment to check the bottom after a spot was selected the ships anchor was secured we started fishing. I was given a hand line without a rod. My catch of this day was 4 fish. On the fishing boat's return trip Pop cleaned all the fish and bought some ice to keep the fish fresh on the long return trip to our home. I remember boarding the train for our return trip and with time to spare Pop Teuchert left the train to get a drink. I'm sitting there alone worried that he wouldn't get back in time of departure. I started to cry. Men sitting nearby came over to console me. I was relieved to see grand pop's return and our return trip to home.

Another time about the middle of 1930 I was able to go crabbing, with my brother Harry and Aunt Millie Teuchert Ingram at Woodland Beach Delaware. A row boat was rented for $2, with our lines and bait which usually was rotting smelly chicken after a few hours we were able to come home with a basket of blue crabs. There were consequences while crabbing there, being bitten by those annoying horse flies. In later years the crabbing at Woodland Beach fell to no crabbing at all. do to water pollution.

OUR STEARNS KNIGHT AUTOMOBILE

I REMEMBER ENTERING THE GARAGE where the Stearns Knight Touring Car was housed the odor for me was pleasant I really liked it and I looked forward to this odor every time I entered the garage. It wasn't much of a building made of frame resting on a few bricks. Not really a foundation, outside stucco finish. Later this garage was replaced by the new owners. On a visit to this home in 2005 the owner mentioned about the garage walls resting on these bricks that I knew about years previously. My grandfather built a long work bench on one side and I marveled how he planned a piece of wood by hand using a wooden plane. When I became older I was allowed to use his tools. I started building small projects bird houses etc. My problem was finding wood to make projects. One source was an orange crate, the ends ad center board were thicker. Pop would sharpen his chisel on an open rotating stone without a resting guard. Pop Teuchert was a great woodworker. At Baldwin's he and my dad were Patternmakers, Wood Joiners with John's son Frank. Years earlier they worked as contractors together at Baldwins why still located in Philadelphia instead of working for hourly they took on bidding. They presented a bid on a article and presented the lower bid and if awarded with the bid made great money doing this.

THE NEW VENTURE RIDLEY RADIO SHOP

WELL THIS WASN'T FOR LONG the Stearns to go it was traded in on a new 1930 Willys Business coupe For Dad's new business called RIDLEY RADIO SHOP located at 23w Winona Ave in Norwood Pa. Where Majestic radios and refrigerators and later RCA radios and appliances were for sale and serviced. He purchased this Willys Coupe with the idea of hauling radios and large appliances by lifting the trunk lid up and sliding it off completely, installed on the floor was a wood deck with hold downs to haul the large standing radios at that time. I didn't like the idea of a business coupe for our family. There was only room for 2 people but many times there were 3 passengers or 4 when I needed a haircut I was driven to Norwood as there was no barber shop in Milmont Park at this time. With the gearshift on the floor made uncomfortable for the passenger in the middle but they survived. My Brother Harry never completed Ridley Park High School, like many others, he may have completed the 9th or10[th] grade like everyone else. Very few completed high school at that time. It wasn't required to get employment.

HARRY ATTENDED RADIO
MECHANIC'S SCHOOL

THIS WAS ABOUT THE TIME of the new business, so Dad sent
Harry to Philadelphia for training on how to service and repair radios.
Harry ended up a good repairman on radios. His shop to do the repairs
was in the back room of the store. Amelia Teuchert Ingram was the
secretary and book keeper for the Radio Business. Her desk was in
the front of the store. To enter the store you ascended 3 steps. There
were several stores of ths type there. My dad rented another one for
storage. I remember being transported to the Store on a Saturday to
get a haircut. I would be waiting for a ride home and about noon I
became very hungry and my father gave me money to cross over to
a delicatessen and buy some rolls and hot dogs. In the back room
where Harry serviced radios sat a little alcohol burner stove to heat
water for the dogs that we were able to eat. Before the business closed
about 1934 Harry brought home an RCA electronic record player
this was our first electronic record player eliminated the old windup
victrola. I liked music and would play the big band popular music on
78 rpm records at that time. I enjoyed the music and it gave me goose
pimples all over my body. My grandfather John said the music was crap
compared to his classics and his waltzes.

THE CLOSING OF RIDLEY RADIO SHOP

WHEN THE STORE CLOSED IN Norwood, do to a downturn in business what was left was moved to the back room of the Milmont Park Post Office and Harry continued servicing and repairing radios for the customers we still held. I remember my brother Harry giving me a demonstration by disconnecting the large separate speaker and hearing the sound coming from the radio's vacuum tubes. The radio repair business fell to a point that it wasn't worth continuing and it was shut down. Harry was able to get temporary employment with the PRT TROLLEY CO removing the ties and rails of the discontinued 76 line that ran from Chester to Darby. After MacDade Blvd was completed Buses replaced the Trolley Car

HARRY'S NEW APPRENTICESHIP
& MILITARY SERVICE

MY FATHER E CHARLES SPEVAK was employed at the Baldwin Locomotive Co since 1901 and was able to secure a position as a Machinist apprentice for Harry.

Harry was hired and received a machinist apprenticeship at the Baldwin Locomotive Works in Eddystone Pa. His starting rate was 25 cents an hour. He did receive the full $10 for 40 hours worked. There were no income taxes for blue collar workers until WW2.Workers paid Social Security tax 1% at that time. He completed and received his journeymen's papers as a machinist. He eventually was operating an 18 ft vertical boring mill when WW2 was declared all employees were obligated to work seven days. Harry was turning parts for the Hoover Dam at this time Later in 1942 Harry married Estelle Bufano and didn't work many weekend and wasn't given a deferment; ended up being drafted. During WW2 about everyone worked continuous without many days off. He was lucky enough by being drafted into the Army Air Force and was sent to Radio School in Madison Wi and eventually Radar School in Boca Raton Fl and last stationed in Albuquerque, NM until his discharge in 1946

OUR FAMILY VACATION TO ATLANTIC CITY

OUR FAMILY DECIDED ON AN outing to Atlantic City during the 1930's well the Willys coupe wouldn't do. Dad had to borrow Uncle Frank Teuchert's 1920's Studebaker touring car for the trip. I remember the trip to Atlantic City traveling over the paved asphalt roads. We had a great time at the amusement pier that once stood near the Million Dollar Pier. It had nice hardwood slides and I remember the rotating disk where everyone tried to stay on but slid off as the table spun. We all had a great time. My sister Alva had a great time there. my sister Aileen was very young then. I just don't remember anyone else from the family being along besides my parents.

THE DEPRESSION

PEOPLE WERE HAVING A HARD time finding employment during the depression and one night our next neighbor who happened to be a unemployed artist as his electric was being turned off for non payment. I was asleep at this time when this happened. I heard that it almost came to gun fire; it wasn't very long after the Bagiltine Family moved out and their home remained vacant probably a Mortgage Foreclosure, my grandfather John and I entered this home and found wine left in a barrel in the basement we took about a gallon. Pop Teuchert gave his grandchildren a diluted sip of wine. Upstairs in the living and dinning rooms of this home the wall's had these beautiful painted murals. Later Cameron Donato & wife and 5 children moved in with his family. Mr. Cameron Donato was a Ridley Township Commissioner a Republican and awarded the contract to haul the city of Chester's trash, waste. He had some of those noisy chain drive Mack Trucks. The Donato's were great neighbors to. I would ride in one of their small trucks when Bobby had a truck loaded to dump. Bobby had a habit of pinching my cheeks. Bobby Donato graduated with my sister Bertha Spevak Embon at Ridley Park High School in 1934 and entered college. He became a teacher and in later years retired as superintendent of the Ridley School District.

THE BUILDING OF RIDLEY TOWNSHIP HIGH SCHOOL

IN 1932 FRANKLIN DELANO ROOSEVELT became president our country was in the heart of the great depression During his administration, he tried to find work for everyone The PWA & WPA were formed by the U S government and were in force. five thousand schools in the country were built during this time and Ridley Township High was one and under construction and the Donato's were awarded a contract for hauling the bricks from the B&O (now CSX) rail siding at Harpers Coal Yard and I remember riding beside Robert Donato on one of these trips to pick up a load of yellow brick for the new Ridley Township High School. Another good event came about at this time and under the WPA. Milmont Park received a complete sanitary sewer system. During all of the excavating and putting up with the mud and dirt we finally were able to do away with those overflowing cesspools. These were filled with peoples ashes and trash. At a later date curbs and sidewalks were installed before all of the roads were finally paved which meant less dirt came into your home.

FAMILY VACATION OAK ORCHARDS DE 1934

IN 1934 DURING THE DEPRESSION the Spevak and Teuchert families saved their moneys for a weeks vacation at Oak Orchards DE. The roads were gravel as we entered the beach. I remember riding with my sister Bertha and her friend Franklin Embon in his 1933 Ford V8. Harry drove Mom with Sister Aileen in the 1933 Willys 2 door coupe, green in color. Grandmom Teuchert and others were driven in Jack Wonderly's old 1920's Hupmobile. The cottage the family rented had a musty order as we entered, after the windows and doors were opened that disappeared. Everything was ok mom and grand mom cooked on a kerosene stove; We went to the general store a short distance away and purchased ice for the ice box. They sold gasoline there to, it was an old non electric gasoline pump. You hand pumped the gasoline up into a measured glass at the top of the pump, it drained by gravity into your car or container. At this time everything was in order until the rain came and the roof leaked. Every pan that was brought along for cooking was now being used to catch the water leaking. After the rain stopped everything became normal. My cousins Frank, Jack and sister Aileen and I enjoyed bathing. My sister Alva 15yrs at this time was leery about the crabs in the water. She wasn't in the water very often.

JOYCE WAS SAVED FROM DROWNING

AN ADJACENT COTTAGE WITH A screened in porch, sat an elderly man, always dressed in a white suite always reading his daily paper. The cottages were close to one another on the board walk. The walk was about 4ft wide. Wooden jetties with a 10 inch board on top ran out from this board walk into the water. Joyce Maguire Quigley 3 yrs Hilda Spevak Maguire's daughter wandered out onto the end of this jetty and fell into deep water, well for the man next door with the white suite saw this happening and rescued her. It appears god was watching and the man in white appeared. He saved Joyce from drowning. We were all very grateful that he was watching. We all had a great time for this week, the Spevak's, Teuchert's and others. Alva was there and became 16yrs old in August, Bertha graduated high school this year and obtained a job as saleslady at the Spears Dept Store, in Chester. She was there for the weekends only.

THE RETURN TRIP TO HOME

NOW IT WAS TIME TO leave and drive home. I rode home in Franklin Embon's 1933 Ford V8. Harry Spevak followed Jack in his Hupmobile. When Jack Wonderly reached Smyrna DE his 1920's Hupmobile car broke an axle. After diagnosing the problem and found it was an axel. Harry continued and reached home with his mother and sister Aileen. He had to find a place to purchase a new axle, while Jack started to remove the old axle. Broken axles were common with those old cars. In those times cars had a compartment for tools usually under the front seat for repairs. Harry was able to purchase an axle and return to Smyrna De and help Jack Wonderly complete the replacement. Everyone riding in Jack's car arrived home in the middle of the night. A trip to southern Delaware in the 1930's the route went straight through the city of Wilmington. Many times on returning from a trip to lower Delaware or Maryland we would stop and purchase donuts at Penny Hill Donuts located on Philadelphia Pike.Their donuts were well known through out and very tasty.

A GREAT FIND

IN LATER YEARS MY NIECE Joyce Maguire Quigley found some B&W negatives that her mother Hilda Spevak Maguire had taken at Oak orchards I looked around on the internet for a place to have these negative made into prints and found it to be expensive. About this time I purchased a new scanner on the market and was able to do this operation. I scanned the negatives and make printed pictures. A great picture of my sister Alva was taken and we were very fortunate that these negatives were in safe keeping. Many times when film is developed and prints are made, the negatives are gone.

THE EMBON COTTAGE

IN AND ABOUT 1934 MY brother-in-law Franklin Embon's mother-Anna C Embon purchased a cottage for $800 at a place called Hollywood Beach Maryland. located on the Elk river adjacent to Port Herman beach. Everyone was excited about her purchase She had it titled in her sons Daniel and Franklin's names, It was small cottage of only 4 rooms 2 bedrooms, kitchen and a living room. and porch. A small addition added on the rear which contained just a flush toilet where you had to carry water to add to the water closet to be able to flush. It had no running water or any electric service. There was an outside well dug with a hand operated pitcher pump where we atained water. The kitchen contained a kerosene stove for cooking and an old fashioned ice box. My first time there I must have been about 12 years old and I was fascinated by the oil lamps burning in the evening hours. My sister Bertha kept a lifetime relationship with some friends when she attended Ridley Park High School. A women named Ruth Hines was one of these friends and later married Frank Hipkins. Frank an electrician and my brother Harry Spevak installed electricity at the Embon cottage. A few years later Anna C Embon had an addition attached to the rear and this was used as family room. later on this addition was made into 2 bedroom The partition between the front bedroom and living room was removed making a larger living room. Franklin and brother Daniel Embon installed an electric pump for a water supply. Many people visited Anna C Embon's cottage and left after having a great time. Later Franklin and Dan bought a boat from Montgomery & Ward with a 7 1/2 hp motor. We enjoyed many boat trips. At the start of WW2 everything became restricted. You needed an identification from the U S government. to operate a boat on open waters during this time of WW2. I was elected to secure this ID card and I went to the U S Custom's House in Philadelphia where I had to apply and did receive a card with my picture and finger print. Prior to me entering the service, in 1942 the boat needed some repair. this boat was a clinker built design and the 2 bottom boards attached to the keel needed replacement. Frank Embon inquired at Montgomery Ward where the boat was purchased and found the boat was built by the Darby Boat Works. We were able to purchase these 2 board from there and they were already shaped for replacement. These board were installed with copper rivets. I invited an old boy scout friend Norman Belak to help me and stay the week at Hollywood Beach. My sister Bertha and her two young children Franklin and Daniel were at the beach for the week to. After a few days my friend Norman and I completed the repairs and managed to have a nice time boating. Later I entered the military service and selected the Air force Norman joined the Navy. During wartime all mail was checked for security. Norman sent Bertha a post card inquiring and joking about the boat that we repaired. He drew a picture of the boat sinking. Well he was taken before the higher up for questioning before being cleared. After ww2 when everything came back to normal. Franklin Embon and Harry Spevak went out for a long boat trip. They traveled to Betterton Beach Md by boat. Weather was getting bad and they had to cross a point in the bay where 3 rivers emptied into the start of the Chesapeake Bay and it was very rough and cold. Harry told Franklin to keep that motor running for us to make it. They managed the return back to Hollywood Beach in one piece ready for some warm clothing. Many great memories of events that took place at the Embon cottage.

MILMONT PARK POST OFFICE

ABOUT THE MID 1930'S MY father was awarded by the U S Government an option to operate the Milmont Park Post Office where people were able to mail and receive there mail.It was a 4th class Post Office and there was no mail delivery until the 1950's Leo Friel was the previuos postmaster and before him was Mrs Scanlon. Harry had the back room where he serviced radios and Millie was hired an assistant Postmaster for a salary of $10 a week. Milmont had no mail delivery, before a post office was established in Milmont Park our mail source was Ridley Park where my father rented a box and ours was #82. I remember the trip to the Ridley Park Post Office. As I got older during the Christmas season I helped my Aunt Millie the ass't Postmaster sort mail during the Christmas rush. In those days it was 3 cents to mail a letter. To send Christmas cards without sealing the envelope it only cost half the cost 1&1/2 cents to mail.

AN EMERGENCY TRIP TO THE DOCTOR

WHEN I WAS YOUNG AND hardly remember I had a peach stone lodged in my throat. I was told that I was driven to Doctors Wolfe's office in Ridley Park, to remove this stone that was stuck in my throat. As I got older we walked over to Ridley Park to get a 5 cent Ice Cream Cone at a place called Milliards that was close to Dr Wolfe's Office. Milliards had a marble soda fountain bar and tables with those old fashioned iron wire chairs. The reason we went to Milliard's was They put as much Ice cream on a cone that was possible and it cost 5 cents and it was Breyers. This was a well known place. Many people from surrounding communities drove to there for their ice cream. I've heard that Milliard's received a prize for selling this amount of ice cream. When we traveled to Ridley Park, as a young child to me it appeared that we were in another world compared to Milmont Park where paved streets, Curbs, sidewalks, Shade trees and squirrels running around. Many large stone homes were in Ridley Park most people were upper class.

MILMONT PARK, RIDLEY TOWNSHIP, DELAWARE COUNTY, PA

MILMONT PARK, PA A SMALL town had unpaved streets, no house numbers (until about 1931) and few sidewalks during the early 1930's. Milmont Park had few houses at that time most houses were located close to the PRT route #76 trolley that began operating in 1900 that ran from Darby Pa to Chester Pa On Belmont Ave to Arlington Ave and Haverford Rd. Being there were no house numbers we knew the names of many people and where they lived. There were a few houses of the bungalow type without a cellar and had no indoor plumbing or running water but they had water from an outside well and hand pump. A kitchen stove for heating and cooking. They also used an out house. Some families raised chickens in their back yard for their personal use. As a young child I remember Ridley Township paving the first street in Milmont Park and it was, Milmont Ave that ran from the Swarthmore Borough line, to the Ridley Park Borough line. Large stones were laid first rolled then sprayed with asphalt coating from a heated truck. Then another coating of smaller stone was applied and rolled with another coat of asphalt. Finally a coating of smaller stone then rolled.

My Dad had to travel to Ridley Park or 9th & Morton Ave, in Chester Pa to get fuel for his automobile. At Ridley Park the Fuel pumps were located between the Curb & sidewalk. I remember the Pure Oil Co station at 9th & Morton Ave in Chester and diagonally acroos the intersection was an A&W root beer stand that was open in the warmer months.

This was before MacDade Blvd was constructed. I remember the construction of MacDade Blvd, the moving of the Frank Teuchert home to make a way for it. After the Teuchert home was moved on to a new foundation, which was made longer where the new enclosed front porch addition, an additional bedroom and new kitchen was constructed. The new cellar was very nice deep with many large windows; maybe the nicest room in the house. I remember traveling along on my tricycle from my home to my Cousins home on Virginia Ave before the MacDade Blvd was in place.

MEETING MY COUSIN'S FRANK & JACK TEUCHERT'S GRANDFATHER

AFTER THE MACDADE BLVD WAS complete and the #76street car was still in operation, before buses took there place, one Sunday morning my aunt Catherine Geraghty Teuchert sent sons Frank, Jack and I to meet her father, their grandfather Charles Geraghty as he departed from the street car at the corner of Belmont and Virginia Aves, he reached into his pocket and gave each one of us a 5 cent piece and said to us (don't let in burn a hole in your pocket.) He arrived for the usual Sunday visit and dinner prepared by his daughter Catherine Geraghty Teuchert. I was always amazed at his neat appearance how was he able to dress in his tailored suit and tie because this man had no right hand. It was told to me he lost his hand as a child, he was riding a bicycle and fell and his hand went under a street car. He and his brother James both usually came for Sunday visits and dinner.

OUR LADY OF PEACE PARISH

BEFORE THE NEW OUR LADY of Peace Church & School was completed for the 1929 school year, our church was the building setting diagonally across from our home at the intersection of Milmont & Belmont Ave. I had learned that my mother Rosa took care of the church alter with placing of flowers etc. The old Church was later renovated to become the sisters of Saint Joseph Convent. The new church had school classrooms on the second floor. I remember the climbing of these metal stairs to reach the second level. The walls of the stairwell were never finished inside the stairwell it was the rough building stone protruding. I entered the 1st grade in 1929 and completed the eight grades. This stone wall was finished at a much later date. We had to ascend the stairs to reach the rest rooms which were located at ground level. You actually went outside to enter another outside door to enter the restroom. The original church was a missionary church under the Saint Madeline Church of Ridley Park. Probably the name of Our Lady of Peace came about when it became a parish.

MOVING OUR LADY OF PEACE RECTORY

MY FATHER HAD PLANNED TO purchase a stone home located at the corner of Baltimore Ave and Hancock St and the deal was never completed. It was later purchased by Our Lady of Peace Church and moved one block up Baltimore Ave to a new location at the corner of Baltimore Ave and Belmont Ave. This became the Church Rectory. The old location from where the house was removed the garage was still there with the existing stone foundation. I heard the garage was used later as meeting place for a boy scout troop. Later this property was sold where a new home now stands.

TIME BEFORE OUR LADY of PEACE

BEFORE OUR NEW SCHOOL WAS completed I remember Loyola & Paul Williams taking me to St Madeline School where they attended. I believe it was a one time thing. We walked down Milmont Ave to the B&O now CSX Railroad we traveled along the railroad to Swarthmore Ave Ridley Park to St Madeline's. school

As young children we went across the railroads quite often being very careful, the lake and the sledding hill were on the other side of the railroad. A great hill for sledding and the lake for ice skating in the winter, fishing in the warmer months. The winter of 1933-34 the Teuchert cousins Frank, Jack and I received Flexible Flyer Sleds and we had a great time, this February was the coldest February 1934 on record a low of -11%. The snow and ice stayed around for along time. The Delaware River froze over, ice breakers were present.

After a day out in the cold winter and at times our feet got wet, just about everyone stopped into the John Teuchert's kitchen to warm there feet and dry Their shoes around the coal stove. Everyone adored the coal stove; it had an oven near the bottom where the heat was and people placed their cold and wet feet and shoes close to it. In the late 1920's ground was broken for a new grocery store at the corner of Belmont and Ohio Aves. I remember the digging of the cellar by using a horse pulling a scoop. This was in the late 1920's I must have been no older than 5yrs. The first proprietor known as the Martin Family operated the store where our family purchased the weekly groceries. Years latter the Campos Family ran the store. Today it is a hair salon. Right across from the new store an empty lot where an old store once stood. This building was probably the 1st grocery store which was moved about one and one half blocks south along Belmont ave and became Nicks barber shop where at that time in the 1930's the price of a haircut was 25 cents.

MY CHILDHOOD FRIEND

MY FRIEND CHARLES VIOLON FIRST lived in a house behind Martin's store. Later the family moved into a new duplex home on Belmont Ave. It had hardwood floors, a built in ironing board in the kitchen wall and the swinging door between kitchen and dinning room. I would visit and play at his home he had the latest toys an erector set was one. I would help him build things. I was a year older then him; his parents would always compliment me after we built something together. This one Christmas time just about everyone got a 2 wheel bicycle I didn't get one. I didn't ask for one and received none. Charles received one and we always rode together on his. He and I were friends a long time we entered first grade at Our Lady of Peace and graduated Ridley Township High School together, enlisted in the Army Air Force together and were together at Miami Beach Fl for basic training and later at Amarillo Air Field for training to become aircraft mechanics. When this training was completed everyone was given a physical examination and those that were eligible went to gunnery school and became flight crew members. This is where Charles Violon and I separated. I didn't pass the eye examination and went for additional training in Seattle Wa Boeing Aircraft factory school.

THE TEUCHERT'S VEGETABLE GARDEN

THE TEUCHERT HOME WAS A 3 story large home placed on a lot 50ft wide x 125ft deep. With an open front porch as it is today. John Teuchert had the porch enclosed as I remember it. This left very little room for a small garden which my grandparents and mother loved to do. They wanted a much larger garden, behind our next neighbor's property was a parcel of open land and we received our neighbors permission to pass upon their land to get to this area. During WW2 gardens were called victory gardens. My grandpa John would be working in the garden early in the morning before leaving for day work at Baldwin Locomotive. They grew many types of vegetables. Every season the garden got larger. At the end of the growing season my grandfather would pickle the green tomatoes, can his hot peppers and hang some in his garage to dry. There was a peach tree and cherry trees.

During the summer season my Mom would prepare a delicious Bowl of vegetable soup from the garden vegetables. I would have a bowl of this soup with a piece of Friehofers golden brown crisp crust bread. I can today still taste the bowl of this soup and bread. Later they would put up by canning tomatoes, peppers cherries peaches Jams etc. Mom would make and preserve relishes, tomatoes, peppers pickles, peaches and cherries for the winter holidays. My Mom was a great cook and baker. She made great yellow cake with her chocolate butter icing, one of my favorites, Struddles, cookies and pies of all flavors. Her cherry pies were my favorite. I remember my Mom buying a crate of fresh strawberries from a huckster, I was disappointed when she cooked them and made strawberry preserves. I loved fresh strawberries. Mom did have appliances that other people did not have. She had an electric waffle iron, an electric sunbeam mixer and Electric toaster. Before the new toaster we had one that set on the gas range burner with four sides toasting 4 pieces at once. She prepared all of her great recipes in this old fashioned kitchen with a coal and gas stove a kitchen sink that hung from the wall with an attached drain board. Occasionally we had homemade waffles made on mom's electric waffle iron. She did have a washing machine and a spare identical one in the garage, At one time the Teucherts and Spevaks lived separately they must of purchased these 2 washing machine then. The kitchen contained soapstone laundry trays where clothes washing was done. We had running water and city gas and electric power was installed at a later time after the house was constructed in 1885. We had loose floor boards on the second floor. How I know about this, I was an Electrician and had to remove floor boards to install wiring. I was surprised that there were no gas lines under the floor boards I have been in houses where Gas was used for lighting and cooking and electric lighting fixtures were attached later. The Teuchert home didn't have gas this came at a later time in this area. They had to rely on oil lamps. The Teuchert's had all of these conveniences, where some families had none. Pop Teuchert insisted for everyone to cook on the kitchen coal stove, he was frugal and mom and grand mom preferred gas, would cook on gas when he was out. We had an old fashioned telephone where the receiver hung along side and when you picked up the receiver you would be connected to an operator and she would ask number please. You would give her the number which was usually 3 digits for a local call and she would connect you. Our number was 383 and later was 140 the Ridley Radio Shop number. When the Radio shop closed in Norwood the 140 number was retained to replace the 383 number. When you wanted to reach someone at a long distance, this became long event. You would give the number and location and she would say (I'll call you back when I have the connection go through). The operator would ring you when the connection was completed. This took one half hour or longer. I found out how long this took place when I happened to be on a furlough and placed a call to Muroc Army Air Field in Ca. Along Belmont St the Keystone phone lines ran and some poles had a red box housing a phone for the police. Before my time police were on horseback. During my time they drove a model A Ford but used the phones to reach headquarters. Later on radio was available, Ridley Twp relied on the Swarthmore police radio. Many families had no phone or auto and they used public transportation or found someone to ride with for work. A few families had a old car for use during the work week and a garage kept new auto that they used on week ends. On Sundays they would dress up and take a Sunday drive. A Sunday drive was great relaxing time back then when traffic was very low. When my brother was employed by Baldwin Locomotive, Harry had a 1929 Desoto roadster. He had riders and charged each one weekly 75 cents to ride up front and 50 cents to ride in the rumble seat. In cold weather everyone wanted to sit under cover.

OUR OLD HOME

MY NEPHEW FRANKLIN C EMBON was able to find the time of construction of the John Teuchert home through records at the Delaware County Court House and it was first recorded in 1885. Everyone is delighted the owners of this home today have renovated it into a show place and I had the opportunity to view the interior with my sister Alva Spevak Draper and her son Norman in abt 2005. I did take some pictures but not enough. This house had 7 bedrooms, 3 on the 3rd floor, 4 on the 2nd floor and 1 bath. The bathroom had wainscot 4ft high painted cream color, an old fashioned tub with legs. I remember my mom Rosa giving me a bath after a summer evening of playing, giving me a bath and getting soap in my eyes. After evening dinner my sisters and brother would make a dash for the bathroom and who ever got in first the others would bang or shout to hurry up. They all had evening events. 1st floor Kitchen everyone ate their meals in the kitchen during week days, The dinning room where dinner was served on Sundays about 1PM and dinner was served on all holidays. Many relatives attended mass at Our Lady of Peace Chuch and would stop by for a visit and were invited to eat the Sunday noon meal. The front room called Parlor and east room family room called sitting rm. A shed where our chess type ice box sat and later the electric refrigerator. As a young child I marveled that it made ice. Our front porch where rocking chairs were for resting during the summer months. As I got older I received my room up on the 3^{Rd} floor adjacent to Pop Teuchert's Rm. My bureau had a few drawers and my wardrobe consisted of 3 shirts, 3 sets of underwear, socks, ties, 1pr shoes and I remember waiting barefooted for shoes that were being repaired, Shoes had leather soles and had a short life.A new pair of shoes came with a breaking in period before they were comfortable to wear. Some psople received blisters. My mother knitted me a maroon wool sweater and it fit perfect and I loved it. I wonder how she was able to find time to do all of these things. We received new clothes at the beginning of the school year I remember receiving a heavy black rubber raincoat with a hood and felt uncomfortable wearing it to school. We received new clothes for Easter and Christmas. Everyone was waiting to see each ones Easter wardrobe. About the later time of the 1930's my cousin Frank Teuchert showed me how to build a Crystal Radio by using a Quaker Oatmeal container to wind a coil around it wire in a crystal and attach earphones. This also required a long outdoor antenna. After I got this radio operating my grandfather John who had the adjoining room, usually left for bed at 7pm would lie in my bed listening to my radio. John liked listening to this radio and used no electric power made him happy because it was on continuously 24-7. I didn't know when my grandfather John slept, As I got older and I was late getting to bed about 1AM he knew exactly when I got in I couldn't cheat on the time. He had a clock on his bureau at the foot of his bed and he knew exactly when I retired. In the front was my father's Photographic room where he developed negatives and made prints. In this room all of the cabinets were painted flat black to avoid reflection of light. At a later time this room was converted back to the 3rd bedroom. His camera had cassettes that held an 8x10 glass film and a 5x7 film. He had this cabinet with many chemicals and I think he made his glass films to because I saw boxes of clear glass 5x7,8x10 etc. I frequented the darkroom to view the negatives. In early years the size of your negative determined the size of your print. On this 3rd fl toward the rear was the windowless attic where things were stored and mom would hang her clothes to dry during inclement weather. Each 3rd floor bedroom had a very nice closet to hang your wardrobe. The second floor bedrooms had very little closet space. On the second floor the front bedroom, I would call the master suite the nicest bedroom on this floor belonged to my aunt Millie and it had an adjacent room for hanging her clothing that we called a sewing room. My parent's room on the west side appeared dreary to me, barely no sunlight. It was cooler during the winter months had no closet. A standing brass clothes rack stood in a corner and a large bureau at the foot of the bed. The east bedroom was larger with 4 windows where Bertha and Alva occupied with a closet and it wasn't deep enough for clothes hangers, it just had hooks on the back wall. The back bedroom did have a small usable closet and my brother Harry occupied this room in his early years until Uncle Bert Teuchert came home to live. No one had a nice bedroom set until aunt Millie bought a complete new Red Maple bedroom set from Tollins Furniture where everything matched. She had a dresser where she could sit and makeup. a new maple bed and bureau. After mom finished doing the laundry all shirts were neatly folded and placed in the bureau drawers. On the first floor the dinning room furniture was the nicest of any room on that level. A round pedestal table a buffet and china closet, It appeared as oak. Many Sunday and holiday dinners were served there. Many pinochle games were played on the dinning table. The dinning room light fixture was a large glass canopy that was later replaced with a modern dinning fixture. The floor had a linoleum rug. The front living room that we called the parlor had the ugliest furnishings an imitation leather set; the floor had a linoleum rug. The ceiling fixture had a large canopy with 4 hanging lights. A piece of furniture that sat in the 90 degree corner for sitting to answer the phone, was a good style but it was covered with that old imitation leather to. A table was placed under the living room fixture with a table lamp with its cord plug in to one of the hanging lamps.This was later moved to a side wall. A picture of the living room is at the end of this document.

NEW LIVING ROOM FURNITURE

IN THE MID 1930'S BERTHA and Alva wanted some new furnishing to be able to invite friend's in. the first thing was remove all of the old furnishings to paint the floor and use a graining method that resembled hardwood when it was finished. A new wool rug was purchased and set down with a 3 piece living room set that was modern. This was a great improvement.

FAMILY ROOM

THE EAST ROOM CALLED, SITTING room (today called a family room) where we had a radio, piano and later a TV a wicker living room set that appeared OK. At a later time a new maple set was bought. My father had a secretary in there to and he kept it locked. He had a locked drawer in his bedroom bureau and I was curious and one day I managed to jimmy the locked drawer. Inside it contained a black jack and some personal documents. The piano set in an recess and behind it a large Christmas mountain stood from the old train setup that my father had built and set up for the Christmas season. I don't remember the old train being setup. It was before my time of remembering. I do remember the remnants the tracks and a nice train station of wood were left as I became older. The mountain was finally given away and this left more room for the piano. The old upright piano at one time was a player piano with the music roll. I remember this. It was later removed and the piano was renovated> People that came around to play it marveled about it's tone.

THE KITCHEN

THE KITCHEN HAD THIS NICE (kitchen cabinet today a collectors item) which had a big bin were the flour was stored on the bottom of this bin was a handle to turn to release flour into a container. This cabinet also had a compartment with a roll top door where spiced were stored, below the porcelain counter top pot and pans were stored. There were drawers and doors too. The kitchen table was enlarged by making and increasing the size of the insert leaf out of plywood making it permanent. With an oil clothe cover that was replaced yearly where mom Rosa made her delicious strudel. This was the first time that I saw plywood. I now have in my possession that I was able to get online the recipe to make this dough and how to stretch it exactly as my mother Rosa Spevak had done The combination coal and gas stove had an oven under the cooktop heated by the coal fire. The top was for cooking. On the right side the gas burners for cooking. Directly above was a gas oven for baking. On the left directly above the coal fire was a gas fired broiler oven which was never used for broiling. It's use was for storing day old bread, the heat from being directly above the coal stove heat dried the bread which mom later ground into crumbs. Milk 10 cents a quart and bread 10 cents a loaf were delivered daily. Before we had electric refrigeration a chest type ice box was in the pantry. I remember when we received the first refrigerator from my father's store it was made by Majestic and I couldn't get over that it made ice cubes. Our perishable things lasted a lot longer. I remember in the severely cold winter months the milk that was delivered to the back door, would freeze and expand out the tops and we would pick these off and eat them. We had French loaves of bread delivered daily by the Friehofer Baking Co; it had a shiny golden crisp crust with a soft interior. Delicious, everyone wanted the ends, my father liked to dunk his into his morning coffee. My Dad E Charles had specially prepared coffee. Milk was heated to the boiling point, then coffee was added until it became tan. I remember him only having this for his breakfast before leaving for work. A later time Bond Bread Co delivered wrapped bread at the front door. At this time sliced bread, was not here, this came at a later date.

BUILDING A KITE

WHEN I WAS ABOUT 8YRS I was interested in building a kite. I asked my grandfather John for some sticks to make a kite. Pop brought me some pieces of wood from his work. I went down to the store and bought a roll of string. I cut these strips of wood to length then making a cross wrapping a string around the perimeter. I laid this on to and old sheet of newspaper, cutting the paper about an inch larger. To fold and glue this to the strings I used flour and water for glue. To complete this kite I used some old strips of cloth for the kite's tail. Then I waited for a windy day to fly it.

THE NATIVITY SET

A FEW LATER YEARS MY grandmother Theresa Teuchert bought Nativity set for Christmas. I saw that no stable came with it. I decided to make one for her. I went out into the fields and found young saplings and cut a few, while still out I gathered some long dried grass for the roof of this stable that I was building, For the floor I found a short piece of Masonite board. I built this for my grand mom and she was overjoyed she made sure it was put away for the following years. I wish that a picture could have been taken

OUR LADY OF PEACE SCHOOL 1929

I WAS ENROLLED AND ATTENDED our lady of Peace School when it first opened and was the first grade to complete the full 8 grades. I felt very uncomfortable in the new school, the classroom windows faced the north, and we never received any sun. It was always cold. When the school first opened in the winter sometimes the rooms were to cold for classes and school was dismissed. At morning recess the boys would be playing baseball and I didn't participate, I just stood against the wall waiting for recess to end, I wasn't interested in playing. I was a slow person and one of the school nuns called me Slovak instead of my name Spevak. I said nothing kept it to myself as I did for years, never responding.

Sister would use the long pole to open the top window a little for fresh air. During the Christmas Holidays, Griffith's Funeral Home from Norwood came to Our Lady of Peace School with a Santa and give each student a box of hard candy. One year all the students went to Woodside Amusement Park for a day traveling in double Decker buses. During another school year all of the students went for a days outing at the Philadelphia Zoo. At the eight grade level I was a member of the Keystone Automobile Club Safety patrol and took all patrol members for a baseball game at Connie Mack Stadium. When the school first opened the rooms had only half of the desks. Sunday masses were 8 am for the school children. When you attended Sunday mass your class sister would sit at the end of the pew. She would keep checking to make sure your body was straight while kneeling not slouched. We knelt on an unpadded kneeler and your knees would be hurting. I made my first communion dressed in white and given a !st communion set. A few years later I was confirmed. In 1936 our pastor Father Reese died from Pneumonia in Chester Hospital.

THE NEW PASTOR

A NEW PASTOR WAS APPOINTED by the Archdiocese of Philadelphia naming Rev I Walter Nall. This was during the hard times of the depression. The parish had an interest debt of about $100 a week and our new pastor was more of a business person and he continued on with the late pastor's Sunday card parties and he received the support of the parishioners of his late parish in Philadelphia. They came down from Philadelphia in bus loads to support him. Father Nall found ways to raise money for the parish. One plan was the Wattis Plan supported by one ot the Philadelphia newspapers, where everyone saved labels from different products and received points which later turned into cash. I believe our parish came out at the top as I read in the newspaper. I remember the block parties in the schoolyard. My aunt Millie Teuchert Ingram was one of the winners and received a table radio. I attended a Sunday night card party in the basement I was playing bingo and won a basket of fruit, after carrying it home, I arose the next morning to find there was nothing left for me. It was put in lunches and eaten. Father Nall was big in sports with the girls and boys ball teams. With his own inherited money he had a tennis court and made swimming pool built for the children. Father purchased a school bus for transporting the students that lived far, and sometimes drove it himself. After his death a ball field was named in his honor. On MacDade Blvd I graduated Our Lady of Peace School in 1937. My grandfather John Teuchert bought me a used Hamilton pocket watch from a pawn shop in Chester for graduating 8 grade. About this time I went from wearing knickers to long pants and I thought that was great.

THE BOY SCOUTS

WHEN I WAS 13 YRS a friend asked me to join the boy scouts with him. We went to the Woodlyn Boy Scout Troop #1 on Fairview Rd. A cabin was already built on John Grace's property over the foundation walls of an old springhouse. The cabin was Constructed from salvaged lumber from old ships being dismantled at The Sun Ship Yards of Chester Pa. This was probably received as a result of one our troop committeemen who was employed by Sun Ship as nurse in the medical dept. He was our troop medical instructor and kept our troop first aid kit in order.The cabin had two mahogany doors reclaimed from the dismantled ships cabins. These doors were excellent 3in thick mahogany, The brass ship hardware that came with it. The cabin was heated with a coal stove but wood was used because our troop meeting lasted only 2 hours, a gas lantern at each end for light. About 1939 used utility poles were obtained by one our troop committeemen an employee of Philadelphia Electric who was able to obtain some used poles to set and string wires for electric power to the cabin for electric. My brother Harry Spevak wired the cabin for light, I really enjoyed this new venture.To become a scout and become a Tenderfoot I had to learn how to tie about 8 different knots, how to display and salute the flag. Learn the 16 points of a compass and other things required to become a Tenderfoot Scout. This knot tying became very useful in later years when I became employed. At the Woodlyn Troop our scout master was great with story telling and leading us with scout campfire songs.

THE VALLEY FORGE PILGRIMAGE

ON THE 22ND OF FEBRUARY 1936 Washington's Birthday the Boy Scout Troops of Valley Forge Council went on a pilgrimage to Valley Forge Our troop rented a bus from the Southern Pennsylvania Bus Co to make the trip to Valley Forge Park Pa. This was a Valley Forge Council yearly event. After the parade was over we were on our own and after visiting the Museum where many relics from the Revolutionary War were on display, we went hiking around the park. There was about 2 in of snow on the ground at this time and the top of it was a hard sheet of ice from rain that had fallen on top of the snow and froze. After sliding down the hills having fun and feeling cold we returned to the bus where it was warm. A friend of mine decided to take a picture inside the bus, the light was dim and decided a time exposure was needed. He steadied the camera on the seat backrest. And when the pictures were developed it appeared that everyone was shivering, The vibrations from the buses engine running to keep it warm was the cause. I had lost my wallet at Valley Forge, I was concerned about loosing my Scout membership card, after a few weeks had passed it was found and mailed to me by another Boy Scout. Another boy Scout doing his turn for the day. As a boy scout I made and placed a railing on our cellar stairs. My mother and grandmother liked it they both said it steadied them ascending and descending the stairs.

CAMP DELMONT

IN 1936 THE WOODLYN TROOP were getting members for a weeks stay at Camp Delmont. Delmont was a name derived from the two counties of Delaware and Montgomery which formed the Valley Forge Council that our troop Woodlyn #1 was a member of. In the summer of 1936 I was able to go for a week at Camp Delmont. I remember the cost was $8.25 for this week. This was the first time in my life away from home and on my own. It was a great event and my cousin Jack Teuchert with me attended to. As we were approaching the camp along the gravel road following the Perkiomen Creek we came to the camp office. Near the office was the screened in mess hall. As we were walking we crossed over the creek on a suspension foot bridge called the bridge of Smiles and ended up on the main campus. We were assigned to a cabin which was open on all sides with bunks. I remember we had these tick bags that we filled with straw for our mattress. The week schedule of events includes swimming in the creek there no lifeguards. They used the buddy system where 2 scouts kept track of one another. Al kinds of crafts and short hikes, The campfire at nights. Crossing the bridge of Smiles each time to dine and all meals were excellent. It was a great event for me.

MY BOY SCOUT UNIFORM

ABOUT THIS TIME MY FATHER wanted the exterior of his office painted. I asked to do it and was given the opportunity to paint it. After it was finished, It did look good.My father E Charles rewarded me and took me to downtown Chester at the Cummings & Glenn Clothing Store where Boy Scout Uniforms were available he purchased a complete Boy Scout Uniform for me. I was so proud to wear this uniform at every Friday night's troop meeting 7pm to 9pm and all other scouting events. The uniform really made me feel that I was a boy scout. I had a great time while in the Boy Scouts. I was a member of the Lion Patrol and our patrol went on some hikes to Rose Valley where Knolton Rd is today it is developed. We would build our campfire and cook and eat our meal before heading back to home. At times all the patrols would go to Rose Valley and the competition was to build a fire and to see who boiled water first. This hike was considered 14 total miles round trip, a requirement for one of our merit badges. I became a Second Class Scout, then First class, Star which requires 5 merit badges and Life Scout 10 merit badges was my highest rank

WOODLYN TROOP CIRCUS & PARADE

IN 1939 OUR TROOP DECIDED to produce and hold a Woodlyn Boy Scout Circus. Other scout organizations said it couldn't be done, well we did it. All of the patrols were getting ready and rehearsing for their acts. The Explorer Scouts were getting ready by building their signal tower lashing the timbers together with rope. They were also putting the Indian tepee up. The tepee was made from old used felt donated by the Scott Paper Co. Explorer Scouts were practicing with their Indian dances, chanting as they danced around as Indian's did. Later on I was selected to become an Explorer Scout and we were invited to perform at events, We put on a show of Indians dancing around a campfire circle shouting Indian talk. This show was usually done during nightfall and we dressed with loincloths and used red brick dust on our bodies. After one of our events at the Sun Oil Field out on Concord Rd it was time to clean up. I started to run toward the shower to remove all of the red brick dust on my body, I fell and landed flat on my back and was able to stand up. I was very fortunate not getting hurt. Our Troop Committee comprised of several senior men were very much involved in our troop. They were the ones who came up with great plans. During the Scout Circus they were up the hill cooking a pig on a rotisserie. We also had a great mothers auxiliary who were there during this event attending to the refreshment stands. Mothers auxiliary also had a party for the troop at Halloween with cookie and apple cider etc. At the start of this event a Parade from Milmont Park to the Woodlyn Troop Grounds was conducted by my father E Charles Spevak Parade Marshall. He rode at the front on a horse that he rented. With all of the proceeds made at this affair it was spent for the scheduled camping trip.

WOODLYN TROOP 1 CAMPING AT THE DELAWARE WATER GAP

THIS EVENT WAS A HUGE success and with the proceeds our Troop went up for 1 week for camping at the Delaware Water Gap. Our Troop bought material to make a tent for each patrol awhile before the camping trip.. The troop bought canvas tarps and we made forms from wood, for a cook tent and another for dinning. I slept in the tent that I made on my mom's sewing machine. Our Troop bought material and plans to make these tents. An adhesive was supplied to fasten the pieces together. These materials laid around for some time with no one taking the initiative to make one. I decided to take this material home and instead of using the adhesive I used my mother's sewing machine and put this tent together erected it and waterproof it. Well another scout saw my tent and he made his tent. His tent was a lot nicer looking than mine. He dyed his material a nice color of green and the sewing of his looked neater to. At the Camp Grounds of the Delaware Water Gap Our Camp was set up adjacent to the main campgrounds where we were secluded. Our program of events included Swimming, Hiking Nature Trails campfires at night. One day we rented enough canoes for a day's canoeing on the Delaware River. A campfire at night with singing and story telling. I had attended many events as a the Boy Scout. Many hiking and camping events. This was a great time in my young life.

RIDLEY TOWNSHIP HIGH SCHOOL

I ENTERED THE 9 GRADE of Ridley Township High School in 1937 as a freshman but I was considered the last grade of Jr high. When I entered the 10 grade I was in the senior high. In my sophomore year I elected the vocational course and entered the machine shop. I wish that I would have taken a general course because in this machine shop training our instructor didn't teach anything at all. We were left unattended and did what we wanted. We did get good instructions attending the Mechanical Drawing Class and the shop Mathematic Class. I wasn't into sports during my school career I didn't dress for Gym. I wasn't very good in sports in running, throwing and hitting. I was embarrassed. When I was young and many years' later people would make fun of something I may have done or said and I was unable to laugh it off like others and this perturb me. I didn't say much, just listened and when I heard something said that I didn't agree with I would sub consciously show disapproval on my face and they would see this and make remarks and I would feel embarrassed.

MY DRIVERS LICENSE AND OUR NEW 1940 PLYMOUTH

IN 1939 I REACHED MY 16th birthday.My father E Charles advance me money to secure a learners permiy to lean to drive an auto. I remember walking over to the next street to Mr Joseph Carney's home our township magistrate to apply. After a short time driving one of my Boy Scout friend's had his license and drove a 1930 Ford roadster and offered to drive me to Chester Pa to take the Pa State driver examination. I passed and received my license to drive a car. Before I was eligible for a License Dad would throw me his car keys to put his car in the garage. His car was out front and I had to drive around to get it to the garage. Every time that I did this it made my day. In 1940 my father traded in his 1933 Plymouth on a new 1940 Plymouth 4dr Deluxe. This auto came with a factory built in heater, the gear shift was located new on the steering column. Dad didn't get a radio installed. The dashboard had a place for one. I asked about it and dad's reply was they are a distraction to driving. It was always in the garage as Dad and Pop Teuchert rode to work with another Baldwin employee. Some times I would be running late for school and I would ask Mom to use the car. Mom would hand me the keys and say be careful. I would drive to school and park adjacent to the machine shop for my friends to see that our family had a new car. Now that our family had a new car and I was at the dating age I was able to use the car when I dated. Now that I was licensed to drive, my mother wanted to shop for groceries at a new location in Darby called THE BIG BEAR located in a former factory building. I remember all cans on pallets stocked high. Mom bought many items at low prices. I remember some prices on cans as low as 10 cents,8cents & 7cents

HARRY RECEIVED A SCARE

MY BROTHER HARRY WAS ABLE to purchase for the first time a used but fairly new 1934 Dodge coupe. Now that I was able to drive and had my license he let me have his car for the 1st time one evening. While I was gone he had heard about an accident That happened at the CSX railroad crossing at Fairview Rd in Woodlyn and a Dodge car was involved. He was worried until a friend drove him down to the accident scene to see and be relieved that it was somebody else. The person was able to vacate before the accident. In my senior year just about everyone went on the class trip to Washington Dc, I and a few other classmates didn't. I didn't buy a class ring. I did get a yearbook. In the year book under my picture read (still water runs deep from Al nearly a peep) In early 1941 my senior year my Brother Harry surprised me by buying a used 1930 Ford Roadster for me. I parked it in the yard and started to take it apart and finally putting it back together. I couldn't drive it until I was able to get tags, which cost $10 then. While in my senior year in 1941 the U S government had already started to draft people for the services in 1939.. At this time we were supplying war materials for England to fight the Germans. Some students left school at an earlier time to work the 4pm to 12am shift. While the senior class were on their Washington Trip, my classmate friends and I decided to skip school and look for a job. I rode with 2 others looking for work. After stopping at several places we arrived up in Philadelphia at the General Electric switchgear plant at 71 & Elmwood Ave. Philadelphia. I had an interview and was hired and I was given a starting time and date. I went outside to find that my friends had gone. Here I was without any money in my pocket for car fare to get home. There was one thing left to do. That is walk, all the way home. About 8 miles plus. I made it, this might have been the furthest that I ever walked. Finally school was ending. Our senior class decided to have commencement outdoors on the gymnasium steps.

Al & Lillian Spevak

Al Spevak

Al Spevak in WWII

John & Theresa Teuchert

Rosa & E Charles Spevak

Al Spevak Family
Al,Al jr,Jessica,Mike,Walt&Jeff

Bernard & Hilda Maguire

Harry Spevak

Estelle Spevak

Franklin & Bertha Embon

Alva & Norman
Draper

Aileen Holmes

Jesse Holmes

Ryan, Jen, Vicky, Dad, Al, Kelly

Jessica Adams & her Family & Dad

The Spevaks, Matheson, Walter...Jennifer & Jessica

The Spevak's Jeff jr, Diane, Dad & Jeff.

THE EMBONS MOVE TO MILMONT PARK

MY SISTER BERTHA AND HUSBAND Franklin Embon rented a house belonging to John Teuchert at 215 Ohio Ave. It was decided to remove all of the paper on the walls, sand the floors and paint some walls and woodwork. The first job was to scrape the paper from the walls. Doing this we found bed bugs just under the paper at door and window openings. It was necessary to fumigate the rooms before any other work was accomplished. The rear bedroom door was removed for convenience this left left a void in the wood james where hinges once were. I found some soft thin wood to repair this. Once completed it was not noticeable. The walls and woodwork were painted, floors sanded and varnished. Bertha was saving enough old wool clothing to send to a company for her rugs. This was near the end of the depression and money was tight. Every little bit helped. After the home was complete everything looked great. At a later date I attended dinner there and Bertha had her dining room table decorated with glowing candles before dinner was served. It was very nice that I was able to help.

MY FIRST EMPLOYMENT THE GENERAL ELECTRIC CO

AFTER THE COMMENCEMENT MY PARENTS drove me to work for the first time on the midnight shift at the G E plant in Philadelphia. I worked there several weeks and. It was very hard to stay awake. I had received a mailing from Westinghouse Electric informing me to come for employment. I had previously applied and was waiting for their reply. This morning I went into the foreman's office And told them I was leaving. He said why are you leaving. I said that I received a call from Westinghouse Electric where I had previous applied. He didn't like me leaving and gave a lot of bull before I left. I couldn't respond to him. This was one of my problems.

WESTINGHOUSE ELECTRIC

THE FOLLOWING MORNING ON THE viaduct at Westinghouse gate there was no pass left for me to enter the plant. The security guard said wait, the personal Manager would arrive shortly. He arrived and I had a conversation with him. He told me that he received a call from GE about me. He said we don't hire each other's employees but being your only learning this shouldn't apply to you. Here is your pass to enter the plant. I started there on the daylight shift helping a machinist named Pete on a horizontal boring mill This machine did work only on large bearings 16 inches plus larger sizes. Production was working 7 day weeks. Being that I was considered a learner i was just working the 37.5 hrs work. After several weeks learning to operate the machine, Pete knew what I was able to do and he wanted some time off to go to New York, he asked the boss for me to run his machine while he took time off. The boss approved and Pete handed me his keys for his tools and I was given the required weekend passes to enter the plant. Pete was a nice person but I didn't like was his love for cigars. He smelled from those cigars. The boss came to me one day and offered me this job on this machine on the third shift as there was an opening on this machine. I accepted and started the dreaded 3rd shift again. It was hard getting any sleep on this shift. I would arrive home in the morning really exhausted. Go to bed and arise about noon or 1pm fully awake and couldn't sleep another wink. In the evening I would go out socializing and came home to go to work and at times I felt too tired to go. I did miss many days of work. Westinghouse employees machine operators worked piecework. I wasn't very fast doing this and was just about able to make my day rate where other employees were able to make 150% on their hourly rate.

MY FIRST HOSPITAL STAY

I WENT FOR MEDICAL CARE about this and my doctor a women after examine me, she suggested that I have my tonsils removed. I got permission from my employer for 1 week absence. I had this done at Chester Hospital and I was taken to my room to recuperate and talking in my sleep. The patient in the adjoining bed said to me who is this girl named Rita, a girl that I had a crush on at the time

HARRY'S 1937 LASALLE AUTOMOBILE

HARRY TRADED IN HIS 1934 Dodge Coupe for the 1937 LaSalle auto. At this time Harry was dating a girl named Estelle Bufano and had a date with her every Friday night. He would be running late. In our house we only had the one bath facility and you had to wait your turn. Harry would give me his car keys to go down to Sun village and pick up his fiancée Estelle Bufano. Estelle lived on a narrow street called Brown St and parking was a premium. I remember entering her home and received a great welcome from her mother. On the way back to our home I had to stop at Millman's dept store in Crumlynne and buy Harry a pair of new shoes. This shoe purchasing became quite often. Harry would buy new shoes for the date, then he would wear the same shoes for work and they would be destroyed. He worked at The Baldwin Locomotive Works machine shop. I never could understand why he never had a pair of shoes just for work.

HARRY SPEVAK & ESTELLE BUFANO'S WEDDING

IN SEPTEMBER 1942 HARRY AND Estelle became married. It was a small wedding. They were married in St Anthony's Roman Catholic Church in Chester Pa. Estelle's sister Marie and I were in the wedding party. A reception was held at the bride's home for the families. E Charles Spevak recorded with 16mm motion pictures. Mr and Mrs Spevak left for trip to Atlantic City NJ. They took residence at the grooms home in Milmont Park, Pa. Some time in November, Estelle received a call about her sister Marie was involved in an accident hit by an auto crossing Morton Ave and it was fatal. I was asked to be one of the Pall bearers. Marie was my age and her death hit me hard to. I remember getting into my car and just driving, thinking about her. From this day Estelle & Harry lived with Estelle's parents home. Harry was drafted into the Army Air Force in 1943. His previouly repaired radios in the family business and was in radio and trained in military radio at an Radio School in Madison Wi and then for Radar School in Boca Raton Fl. He was sent to an Air Base in Va. While there he and some other men were sent down to Atlanta, Georgia to do machinist work. When Germany Surrendered in 1945 Harry was immediately called back to active duty. He served his remaining time at an Air Base in Albuquerque NM before being discharged in1946

THE MILITARY DRAFT

LATE IN 1942. MY AUNT Millie the postmaster gave me my mail and the dreaded letter from the draft board which was located in Sun Village, Chester, Pa. My neighborhood friends received theirs to. I didn't want to be drafted into the Army and carry a gun. I thought maybe the Navy would be the service for me, my brother-in-law Norman Draper was in the Navy. I met a close friend Armond (pip) Baroni and told him my plan. He said Al, lets not enlist in the Navy. He was working at the Navy Yard in Philadelphia at this time and knew something about the Navy. He said lets join the Army Air Force. He and my other friend Charles Violon and I all decided to enlist in the Army Air Force.

ENLISTING INTO THE ARMY AIR FORCE

THE 3 OF US TRAVELED to the Philadelphia Customs house to enlist. After completing all of the paper work, we were sent to the national Guard Armory on Lancaster Ave for physicals. After the physical and reporting back to the U S Customs House, we were given an order to be at the Customs house on Friday morning November 27 1942 Friday following Thanksgiving. On this day we took the oath and were sworn as U S Military. My brother-in-law Franklin Embon was present as he was always there for me. We were taken to the B & O train station now called CSX for the trip to Camp Meade Maryland. We could view Armond's home as we were passing by. We arrived at Camp Meade at dark and were taken to the Army mess hall and given a meal of Beans, hot dogs & rolls. We were then taken to a 2 story barracks and given bed linens and quarters for the night. When morning arrived; I heard this (get the hell up and get the f--- up and outside for roll call). I thought to myself, what have I joined after hearing the foul language. We were here for about a week getting our clothing gear and immunization shots. It was really cold this year, winter of 1942-43

MIAMI BEACH FOR BASIC TRAINING

WE WERE TAKEN TO UNION Station in Washington DC by bus while waiting for our train to Miami Beach Fl for basic training. After a long wait the guys flopped down and fell asleep on the station benches, well by the time that I looked around there was no place vacant. I was dead on my feet just waiting for our train; I figured that after It arrived I would at least get some sleep in the Pullman car.. One of our soldiers said (the train had arrived) and to my surprise it wasn't a Pullman just one of those old Pennsylvania day coaches, the worst cars that I ever rode in while traveling. After sitting up with a terrible ride south to Miami Beach we finally arrived and taken to a hotel called the Metropole on the 6^{00} block of Collins Ave in Miami Beach Fl. This hotel was a small 3 floors one not very old. All of the rugs were removed and each room had a chest of drawers and army bunk beds. We were shown how to arrange every peace of clothing. Everyone was given a drawer, and every piece had to be in a special order. The following days we were marching singing a song called jolly jolly six pence. Some guys were replacing the lyrics with sexy ones and the drill instructor put a stop to that. after more marching, calisthenics etc we started getting more immunization shots. Well I didn't like getting these shots with their procedure which was standing and as you walked by boom a shot in your arm. We had our meals in the shutdown restaurants taken over by the U S Government operated by the Army Air Force. When we went for dinner we were required to carry our own canteen cups. This one evening at dinner they gave us this chocolate drink and when we put it to our mouth started to drink it was horrible we were unable to drink. It appeared that it was just water and chocolate. The mess lieutenant found this out and he made all the cooks in the kitchen to get a full cup and sit down and drink it. I remember my first time doing Kp. We were awaken early one morning and taken to a large hotel fr Kp. We were treated kind of rough probably because we were new recruits. At night there was a night club almost across from our hotel. Everyone was served, I believe all military persons were served everywhere I was never refused alcohol before I became 21 years. There were no civilians in sight. Weekends and evenings were off and we could do just about anything and that amounted to bathing. The water was fine and warm. I made a bad decision; I decided to take up smoking and had this habit for 30 years before quitting. I have pictures of me taken at the beach and on the roof of the hotel. I went to a photo studio and had my first portrait taken in my uniform. My dad E Charles Spevak commented about this picture saying (the photographer produced a very good portrait.) As I celebrated Christmas of 1942 in Florida; I felt a little homesick during this time. Usually At Christmas at home it was cold and at times snow. Our outfit didn't get the required 6 weeks of basic training. We shipped out before completing training. We left before the New Years day. The day that we left Miami Beach the weather was very stormy and chilly.

ARRIVING AT AMARILLO ARMY AIR BASE

JUST BEFORE NEW YEARS WE left by train with Pullman cars this time we were able to sleep for the trip to Amarillo Texas, for B17 Airplane Mechanics School. We arrived there and it was a nice sunny mild day. I was told that we missed a snow storm and I didn't see snow, but around one the building's in a shaded area lay some snow.

We were marched to our new barracks. The barrack appeared very shabby with a roll type of covering and had 4 guy wires on each side for wind supports. You had to be careful during the dark hours to avoid running into them. These were temporary for wartime. The barracks had 2 gas fired standing automatic unit heaters nicely spaced and the barracks were warm and toasty.. It had a nice floor, windows for daylight, double bunks and a foot locker. I manage to get a lower one. Our washroom was close by. Here we go again, school is around the clock and we are stating on the 12 to 8 turn. Our first classes were across the airfield to a hanger owned by Braniff Airways. We arrived there after the long cold walk and entered the cold hanger. It was ice cold for heat some 8in pipes stood upright with a gas flame. For any warmth you had to get right close to these heaters. They had some old antic B18 planes there. We didn't get anything of value there. It was much better on our next class location.

THE ARMY HOSPITAL

WHILE ON THIS TURN BEFORE turning in to bed one day I ate a chocolate candy bar and drank a bottle of coke. We were awakened about 10:30pm for the night turn. I felt ok until I stood up. A sharp pain in my lower stomach erupted. I ended up on sick call and taken by Army ambulance to the Base Hospital. Doctors came in and examined me with a rectal examination and a blood test was prescribed for appendicitis which proved negative my pain ended by the morning. They diagnosed it as an obstruction which cleared up.I was hospitalized 4 days before being discharged. One day I looked out the window to the adjacent ward and people were getting out of ambulances then army truck loads we later found they were being treated for food poisoning. They had some delicious ham for dinner. They kept me there for a few days under observation then released me. This washed me back about 3 classes to another class. We had calisthenics' when we weren't on day classes. I didn't mind this, but it was completed with a long run. I and some others dropped out. My problem I developed a pain just under my lower left rib cage every time that I ran a great distance. I should have gone on sick call. I did gain about 10 pounds during this exercise program and fell back to my normal weight of 170lbs when all of calisthenics stopped. On our days off we went in town to Amarillo Texas. There wasn't much to do there. One time that I was going to town a friend asked me to take a check that he received from his former employer. GM and he asked me to get cash for it while I am in town. Well I just about visited every bank and had conversation with every bank manager without any success. He had to cash his own check.

While in Amarillo for my first time I received a haircut done by a women barber, this was the first time for me. This appeared strange to me. This base was big with Post Exchanges, Churches, Movie theaters, etc. I bought my first fountain pen at one of the PX's. It was a Shaffer, (before ball points)now I was able to write home. One part of our training was for one week to go out into the field and repair Airplanes. Sleep in pup tents. This was a new experience for the soldier in my tent. With my knowledge of camping learned as a Boy Scout; I knew how to pitch a tent and to dig a little ditch around for rain. It did rain and hard, our tent was ok. No water came in. Many other tents got water inside. It was decided that we move into newly erected squad tents with cots were installed for us. Here we were stomping around the mud in our tent floor figuring out how to get undressed for bed. I believe we removed our muddy shoes and undressed while standing on the bed and dressed in the morning putting our shoes on last. The later part of May our class completed with training and everyone was given the rank of corporal. and waited for shipment. Soldiers with 20-20 eyesight went to gunnery school to become B17 crew members. Soldiers that didn't qualify which I didn't because of my eye sight, ended up being transported to Seattle Washington for advanced training at the Boeing B17 Aircraft School, in Seattle Washington.

AT SEATTLE WASHINGTON

OUR BASE IN SEATTLE WA was small to accommodate about 200 hundred soldiers. It was located in a residential community with just average fencing. Classes there lasted about 6 weeks. The mess hall was operated by civilians. This was good we didn't have any KP duty. After classes on night we were given a tour through a Boeing aircraft assembly plant. All that I saw were fuselages one after another and being built by women. The advanced B17 bomber training was very good. On the B17 must things were operated electrically and I scored very well in the electric examination. This probably was why I chose the Electrical field for my profession after military service. After completing the school we waited to ship out, there was a backlog and we had to wait on shipping out to Salt Lake Air base a replacement center. They decided to give us the needed basic training that we never completed at Miami Beach. We marched up to an area where we were able to shoot some rifles and guns. After this training and waiting in our barracks for shippment a few of us were horsing around and one guy picked me up under my arms and suddenly I felt very warm and uncomfortable I ended up in the hospital again where my temperature was taken and I had fever. When you developed a fever bed rest was prescribed. I was in bed for a few days and given treatment before being released. At advanced B17 Boeing Aircraft School we were able to get into the city of Seattle Wa. Quite often on weekends. This city is similar to San Francisco Ca, it's hilly. I asked a civilian how about winter snows, his reply there is no winter snow along the west coast. Well I heard this past winter 2011 Seattle did get some snow. The eastern part of Washington has hard winters and snow where the western part of the state is mild. We always went to this recreation area nearby for free lodging. And it had games and outdoor games to. This one weekend 4 of us decided to take a boat trip from Seattle to Victoria Canada. This was quite a trip being wartime submarine nets were in place and had to be opened for river traffic then closed. After arriving in Victoria Canada it appeared that we were in the 1920's. All the autos were 1920's models. There wasn't anything happening there being a weekend. We manage to ride a street car from one end to the other end. We had dinner in a restaurant and it was confusing on the money exchange. By this time it was time to leave and we boarded the ship for our return trip to Seattle Wa.

SALT LAKE CITY AIR BASE
& HARVARD NEB.

FINALLY WE SHIPPED OUT TO An Air Base in Salt Lake City, Utah for assignment. It was hot at the Salt Lake Airbase. One day while waiting for our assignment I heard that we were scheduled for a hike and for everyone to bring along their gas mask. They needed 4 volunteers for duty and I volunteered. I was told to, never volunteer, but I took the chance. The four of us were put on a truck for delivering ice for a nearby post, that turned out very good. After this job was completed the driver of this truck took us up on top of a mountain where it was cool and a beautiful view of Salt lake City. The driver said he made this trip quite often.

HARVARD AIR FORCE BASE

I FINALLY RECEIVED ORDERS TO ship out to Harvard Air Base, Harvard Ne and assigned to the B17, 447 bomb group and the 711 bomb squadron. Our squadron symbol was 2 dice on our B17 bombers. The trip by train from Salt Lake to Denver. This train trip on the Western Rio Grand lines was one of the most beautiful train rides that I had ever taken. The train traveling through the river gorge. traveling around many turns and through tunnels the largest one was the Moffat tunnel 7 miles long. At times looking out you would see the locomotive at your right or left side. We finally arrived at Harvard Air Base located in corn country. This was a new air base ground leased from a farmer. with new hangers, new barracks and mess halls. In this part of the country coal was used for fuel for heating the barracks and for cooking in the mess hall. We were waiting for all of our new B17 Flying Fortresses to arrive not able to do anything. I was awarded the rank of Sergeant here. Our planes did finally arrive.

MY FIRST FURLOUGH

ABOUT SEPTEMBER I WAS GIVEN a furlough to leave for home for the first time. I was able to get bus transportation to Grand Island Ne. After 10 months of training I boarded a Union Pacific train for bound for Chicago at Grand Island Ne. While on the train the soldier sitting next to me opened a box with fried chicken and offered it to me. It was delicious. It is strange that your mind can remember thing from years back. Arriving in Chicago in the morning. I boarded a Pennsylvania R R train at 12pm leaving for Philadelphia and I arrived in Philadelphia the next morning. I took a rail car to Macdade Blvd, Collingdale, than boarded a 76 bus to Milmont Park Pa, Pop John Teuchert was the first one to meet me being the early riser. that he was. I could see he got a little emotionally a tear coming from an eye. I finally was able to be with my parents and siblings during my first time home after ten months. This being September 1943 the climate was still quite warm Dad took 16mm motion pictures in the back yard of me in my uniform with my sister Alva Draper, her son Norman and my sister in law Estelle Spevak with daughter Marie. While at home I went to the ration board located in Ridley Park Pa, presented my furlough papers and received some stamps for food and some gas stamps for the auto. My mother Rosa couldn't get over the amount of food stamps given to me. Yes everything was rationed during WW2 food clothing, shoes, wages, rents and all prices were frozen for the duration. I enjoyed my mother Rosa's cooking after 10 months without it. After home for about a week and after the long train ride, I returned to my base in Nebraska.

MY FLIGHT ABOARD A B17

EACH SQUADRON WAS SENDING 2 B17 planes and crews at a time to Galveston Air Base for bombing and gunnery practice over the Gulf. I was one of several to be selected from my squadron #711 to go there as a mechanic to service our 2 planes. I flew down in one of the new B17 model "G" planes. They flew below 10,000 ft so that I was able to go. This was my first time aboard a bomber. The weather was warm and sunny during the flight. It was a great experience. I crawled back into the tail gunner's compartment for a great view of the trailing B17's behind us.WE arrived at the Galveston Air Base and the stay lasted a few weeks. I did manage to get to the town of Galveston for some night life. After the training was finished we were getting ready to return to Harvard Air Base. I remember 2 mechanics went awol their homes were a few hundred miles from Galveston. We were in an old B17 tow target plane waiting for take off and I noticed we were taxing back to the line. Our flight was cancelled; the weather was bad at Harvard NE. This was good for 1 mechanic that was able to return. The fallowing day it was decided we could fly to Pueblo Co and stay there overnight while waiting for the weather to clear in Harvard Ne. While getting instructions to land in Pueblo Co one of our landing gears didn't extend down. I was selected to enter the Bombay compartment where I was able to crank it down manually. We bedded down for the night. The following morning after boarding the old B17 tow target plane again we finaly did take off for Harvard and getting ready to land in Harvard Ne I had to crank the landing gear down again and we landed safely. The remaining weeks there. I was scheduled for dreaded yellow fever shot, well all talk going around about this shot got me nervous.

I went and received this shot and passed out. I dreaded getting shots, today in my older age it doesn't bother me I had suspicions that this may have been the reason that I was left out of the 447 bomb group that left for England.I wished that I could have gone to England with them. I felt left out. I was temporary assigned to the base unit awaiting reassignment.

REASSIGNED

I WAS ASSIGNED TO THE Harvard base unit waiting reassignment I being a sergeant in charge of a group of men while awaiting assignment. A friend and I went into the town of Hastings one night for some entertainment, while there we had some drinks and returned to the base. We both awoke in the morning to find the barracks empty and the clock at about 8am. Did anyone try to awaken us, I never had a chance to ask anyone; I was downgraded back one grade to corporal and placed on kp for the remaining days at Harvard NE. It was a relief to leave Harvard Air Base after the downgrade and the continuous kp duty. We left Harvard Ne for Idaho

382 BOMB GROUP

I WAS REASSIGNED TO THE 382 bomb group at Pocatello Idaho. This was a B24 Liberator group. It was a relief to get away from Harvard Air Base. When we arrived in Pocatello Id the weather was ICE COLD with a hollowing wind. While waiting in our barracks for orders, a thought in my mind was that I wouldn't survive in this cold weather. I never experienced weather like this before. The airplane mechanics stationed there wore sheep lined clothing jackets and pants. Well to my delight I heard from one of the mechanics, that we would be leaving in a few weeks to a warmer place. I never did get assigned to a unit while in Idaho

MUROC ARMY AIR BASE

WE LEFT BY TRAIN FOR Muroc Ca in the Mohave Desert. When we arrived at Muroc it was a desolate looking place, It appeared that A fighter group were there previously. There was no vegetation here. We arrived in December and the weather was cool and the rainy season was just starting. A few weeks of rain during this time of the year with ice forming on puddles during the nights. During the summers the temperature reaches 110 degrees in the afternoons. Daytime flights were postponed until the evening hours. It was so hot that if you walked on a wing your shoes would stick. At night it is so cool blankets are used for sleeping. No mosquitoes were present. They did have a nice swimming pool for us to cool off during the oppressive summer heat. At one time dust storm came upon us and this storm was identical to the storms that I observed in those western movies scenes with the tumbling tumble weeds. Today this base is called EDWARDS AIR FORCE BASE, which was about 110 miles northeast of Los Angeles. This area was selected with its weather for year around flying. Our new operation here was training replacement B24 bomber crews for combat and our mission was to maintain the planes for training. The base came up with a new plan for servicing and repairing the B24 planes.

OUR NEW GROUP 421 AAF BASE UNIT

OUR OLD GROUP NUMBER 382 Bomb group was changed to 421 Base Unit We no longer assigned to a particular plane. The new plan was called production line maintenance, and one of the 4 squadrons was eliminated which one the 436,437,438, or439 The 437 was the one selected for elimination probably from a hat and the men were distributed amongst the 3 remaining squadrons It happened that I was originally assigned to the 437 and this one was eliminated. I was assigned to the 438 and our squadron ended up with 2 mess sergeants and they happened to be brothers and Italian. One came from 437. We had great meals prepared by them. Some men were assigned to inspections, I was assigned to an engine crew our position was to replace B24 engines. There were five engine change crews of 4 men each and we took our turns. sometimes we had days without any engines to be changed. Some mechanics were assigned for propellers and others assigned for turbo superchargers. I was disappointed that I was transferred to the 382 bomb group. I wanted stay with the 447 bomb group but as time went by I got over this, with all of my trips to Los Angeles, Hollywood and other communities, everything turned out great. I had a great time in California for the remaining two years of my military service.

A MEETING WITH COUSIN JACK
TEUCHERT IN LOS ANGELES

SOMETIME AROUND DECEMBER 1943 OR January 1944 I was able to meet with my cousin John Teuchert a Marine of 4th Marine Division from Camp Pendleton Ca we met in Los Angeles Ca and we were able to spend the weekend together. We visited his great aunts Catherine and Mary Ellen Geraghty who lived in Los Angeles and had been there for years. I saw them listed in the 1920 census of Los Angeles, Ca. We had dinner there. We later went to the Hollywood Palladium Dance Hall where one of the great bands were playing there. Tommy Dorsey I think. I never danced but did like the music and spent my time at the bar. Jack and I had an 8x10 portrait taken together.This portrait eventually got lost. Later on Jack came up to me and said he found a place for us to stay the night. Jack very out going made conversation with one of the band members was given an invitation for us to stay in one of his spare rooms for the night. Jack returned to his base and a short time later and we were never able to meet again Jack Teuchert shipped out into the Pacific theater with his unit for combat.

MY MANY TRIPS TO TOWN

I MADE MANY TRIPS INTO Los Angeles on my time off. My first trip to Los Angeles was by way of an army truck. Well that wasn't very comfortable. It was windy and cold riding in the back. After arriving in Santa Monica Ca. We arrived at a free reservation for service men. I made several trips to Hollywood Ca by hitching a ride and usually stopping at particular Italian Restaurant in Hollywood Ca for a spaghetti dinner with a basket of bread and a bottle of beer. My first trip into Los Angeles I ended up in a bar called The VICTORY INN, it was located down in a basement under a store in the center of Los Angeles. It had a very nice wide entrance stairway I visited there quite often meeting women and some were it. A popular song during WW2 called (there either to young or to old) pertaining to the men. With our population of about 125 million there were 15 million in uniform. Girls were looking for men of their age. On one of my later trips into Los Angeles it happened to be July 4th 1945 the European War had ended. I met a girl at another bar called the Oasis we got acquainted and with a Navy guy were invited for dinner with her friend at their home, After dinner my date and I went to the coliseum for the 4th of July celebration. There was a bus service from our base to LA, this wasn't very satisfactory with our schedule. The better way was to get a ride from the base into Lancaster then hitch hike the rest of way. One friend went home on furlough to New Orleans and drove back in his 1938 Buick Car. I enjoyed many times visiting in los Angeles and Hollywood Ca. I managed to ride into LA with him a few times. Gasoline was rationed during war time and for him to gas up we acquired the gasoline out of the drums located on the line. This gas was only 73 octane used for cleaning the aircraft engines. It was there for the taking until locks were put on each drum. So we would have to obtain gas from the planes for our cars.

LONG BEACH

I WAS ABLE TO VISIT some people at Long Beach Ca. The Czinger family at one time lived in Milmont Park Pa directly across from Frank Teuchert his wife Katherine and sons Frank & John on Virginia Ave. Mr. John Czinger worked at the Navy Yard in Philadelphia, Norfolk Va and finally Long Beach where his son John had found residence to. Mr. Czinger was employed in the Long Beach Navy Yard as a boiler maker and was very hard of hearing, at the time our technology was in its infancy and he wore a hearing aid that hung from his neck about the size of today's large remotes. Their daughter Irene lived their to. I made several visits there, one time it was over the Thanksgiving Holiday. We motored to a turkey farm, picked out a live turkey and it was killed and cleaned while we waited. While I was in California I visited many towns Los Angeles, Hollywood, Santa Monica, Pasadena, San Bernardino, Long Beach and El Monte etc. After a long wait I finally received my Sergeant rank back. Why it took so long, there were no openings for advancement. While At Muroc Army Air Base a friend mechanic that I worked with decided that he didn't care about working on aircraft and was able to get a job in the office. I believe he put in a word for me to attend an engine school as an opening came available.

WRIGHT AERONAUTICAL ENGINE SCHOOL

I WAS SELECTED AND SENT to Patterson NJ to attend the Wright Aeronautical Engine School for a 6 week course. I was given a course in the Wright R26oo Engine. The train trip to Patterson was a little different this time. From Chicago I went by way of the New York Central RR to New York City. This train had a Club Car where alcohol was served and I remember drinking scotch. While stationed in Patterson I was able to come home to Milmont Park on weekends to visit my parents. I took a bus to Newark NJ boarded a PRR Train to Chester then a bus to my home. While there the European War had ended. After the training I returned to Muroc Air Base and found that all of the B24 planes were gone and replaced with B29s. I became a Staff Sergeant crew chief working on B29's. My duties as a Staff Sergeant didn't last very long.After VJ Japan had surrendered. I wish that I was able to be in Los Angeles on VJ day. From what I read in the Los Angeles paper everyone had a great time. I and many other military personnel were stuck on duty during this time. WW2 was declared over after the Japanese surrender the military started to discharge personnel. My enlistment read the duration plus 6 months. Well later on soldiers were being let go on the point system. I had only about 36 points for my 36 months of service and I needed 45 at that time. New rules came out that anybody with 3 years service 36 point was eligible for discharged. I was excited waiting for my name to come up on the Squadron Bulletin board. Then it happened my Master Sergeant said AL your name was posted. I went down to read the posting and I saw that It wasn't for discharge and my named and 11 others were to report 13 hrs (1pm) to Mess Lieutenant ----- for duty.

SERVING IN THE MESS HALL

WE ARRIVED AT 1PM AND were told we were going to be cooks in the mess hall kitchen there was a shortage of cooks. some have gone for discharge. We countered, we're not cooks and the lieutenant said that he wasn't a Mess officer but an engineering officer. He to was out his field to and said we would be cook's helpers. Two jobs were open for Kp pusher. I took one and another guy from New York took the other Kp pusher job to assign kp's for their duties. A Kp pusher's additional job was to make the coffee in one of those large coffee urns. I wasn't given the right information on the amount of coffee for the large urn. My first time on making the coffee was a bust. It was weak.. Kp's duties were able to select jobs on their time of arrival, first there had first pick. Cleaning pots, and pans were usually left for the last arrival. Kp pushers hours were from 12 noon until after Dinner cleanup then from 6Am until 12 noon, then the following 24 hrs off. this job did have some benefits.. One evening after dinner, A few of us were drinking beer in our quarters when someone said fried chicken would be great with the beer. I said no problem, I took two guys over to the mess hall and we fried some chicken and before leaving the mess hall making sure we left everything in order. I just don't remember the amount of time I spent in the mess hall before I received orders for discharge. The 2yrs plus that I spent at Muroc Army Air Base now (Edwards Air Force Base) I had a great time meeting and becoming friends, with many people When WW2 finally ended everything stopped all manufacturing. People were laid off. unemployment lines were long as we observed in Los Angles while on leave. MY FURLOUGHS HOME After remaining in Muroc Air Base for just over 2 years and having 2 furloughs of 15 days plus 7 days travel time. My train trip home to Milmont Park Pa to quite some time. I would travel to the Los Angeles train depot with my luggage buy my ticket which cost about $75 round trip, board the union Pacific train for Chicago at 6Pm, the following evening we were in Salt Lake city Utah. The following evening we arrived in Omaha Ne. The next morning we arrived in Chicago. Leaving Chicago about 12 noon I arrived in Philadelphia the following morning, just about 3 ½ days one way. My name finally appeared for discharge from the service I was shipped out on the Santa Fe RR to Chicago then for discharged from the service at Wright Patterson Air Field Ohio on January 29 1946. Before leaving for home all stripes were sown on our uniforms and we received the discharge button called the ruptured duck. That I have with all my medals today.

ARRIVING HOME AFTER 3 YEARS

AFTER ARRIVING HOME I HAD to do a little shopping for civilian clothing. When every one of the family members arrived home from WW2, we all came together in our military uniforms one Sunday for motion pictures taken by my father E Charles Spevak. These pictures are in the family films. When the war finally was declared over, everything stopped all of people that were employed making war materials were laid off. The lines around Employment office circled city blocks. This happened while I was still in California. After arriving home I took a trip to the Westinghouse MFG looking for work but there was nothing there.

FIRST MEETING OF LILLIAN MY WIFE

I ATTENDED A PARTY AT one of my friend's James Sykes's home of Woodlyn Pa and first met Lillian Johnson for the first time. And she made a big impression on me. One reason that I liked about her was she was quiet like me and we both never danced but loved music. She lived in Chester at 1111 Chestnut St at this time with her parents Jesse & Edna Johnson, brother Walter and sister Betsy, At one time the Sykes Family Lived next door to her and later moved away. Lillian worked as a cashier at the Edgemont Beef co located on Edgmont Ave in Chester. Mrs. Sykes stopped in there one day and recognized Lillian and was asked to do some ironing for her. Lillian liked to iron clothes and she done this regularly. An automobile was at a premium after WW2. Price control were still in effect. My brother Harry and I were looking to purchase a car. We went to many dealers we couldn't find anything we liked. There was nothing much around, To buy anything it was at a premium because of ww2 price controls were still in effect and you paid extra under the table. A former neighbor came by with a 1937 Willys for sale, An identical car that I owned prior to entering the service. I bought it and it was painted with a brush. Harry and decided to spray paint it with lacquer. It required a clean strip. We bought about 2 gallons of paint remover and removed, the layers of paint, repaired some rust spots and spray painted it maroon with cream wheel rims. It looked very nice. We than took some jobs painting cars which I didn't like doing, my job was a lot of hand sanding and compounding after painting. I wanted some good employment and I applied back at Westinghouse Electric and was given a job in another dept on the dreaded 12 to 8 shift. The dreaded 12 to 8 I worked there a few months and it wasn't working out and I and some others were let go. I did have machine shop training in high school. In the military service getting training at the Boeing Aircraft school I did very well in electrical. And decided an electrical field would be my profession.

PENNSYLVANIA ELECTRICAL
SCHOOL of ELECTRICITY

I APPLIED FOR TRAINING AT an Electric school in Philadelphia called The Penna School of Electricity under the G I bill of Rights. I attended this School 4 hours daily from 8am to 12 noon. In the meantime I was deeply in love with my wife Lillian. We went and got married at Elkton Md and lived with her parents for a short time.

OUR FIRST CHILD

OUR SON ALFRED WAS BORN on my birthday. January the 16 day of 1947. My son Alfred had trouble feeding and with our doctor's care we tried all kinds of formulas without any positive results. Our family doctor sent us to a local nose and throat specialist. We took our baby Al there and his diagnosis was there was nothing wrong, he would grow out of it. Our family Physician was outraged after receiving the report.. She tried to make an appointment for us with a specialist in Philadelphia at Children's Hospital of Philadelphia. He was booked solid. We were told and able to receive his service through the Hospital Clinic. We drove one weekday and they were able to open his clogged nose path. While he was feeding he couldn't breath through his nose, this was the reason for his problem.

WE FINALLY HAD OUR OWN PLACE

WE WANTED OUR OWN PLACE an apartment in the William Penn homes in Chester was available. Me being a veteran and my wife's Mother Edna was able to get this for us, being a committee women in Chester. In 1947 we were given a one bedroom apartment at the William Penn Public Housing at 302 Gartside Ct on the 3rd floor. My wife Lillian and I were happy that we now had our own place. Now we needed furnishings. WW2 was over and companies were getting back to producing products that they made prior to the war. My wife Lillian had a nice bedroom set. We were able to purchased a cheap 3 piece maple living room set and a kitchen table and 4 chairs. We needed a refrigerator and none was available at this time. We managed to get an old ice box, Yes we had an ice delivered until we finally were able to purchase a new refrigerator and a Maytag ringer washer. The first time that she used the washer and laundered some sheets to dry outdoors they disappeared. the apartment was in a fire proof building. The floors concrete painted gray. The walls had a plastered sand finish painted off white. A kitchen adjoined the living area, it had a large combination sink with a large laundry tub. The only things of wood were the bathroom and bedroom doors. The bathroom had no shower facilities just a tub for bathing It was getting close to Christmas of 1948.

OUR FIRST CHRISTMAS 1948

I WAS AT THE SEARS Dept Store in Chester and they had this Lionel train on display. I thought this would be great under our tree for our first son's Christmas, After purchasing the train, I made a 4ftx8ft platform for the train and tree. The platform that I made had lighted model houses and I painted it green for grass. It looked good. My wife Lillian decided to drape a product called angel hair over the tree. It looked good to but our baby Al crawled onto the platform and received a dose of this itchy angel hair. That was the last time for angel hair. The following Christmas we had moved into a 2 bedroom apt and there was no room for the train display. I did set this up in my parents living room. While living in the new 2 bedroom apartment I received my Pennsylvania WW2 Veteran State bonus of about $300.

OUR FIRST TV

TELEVISION WAS JUST GETTING STARTED and very expensive. RCA came out with a new 10in table Black & White TV for a reduced installed price of $170. We purchased this TV and that included an installed outdoor Antenna. After arriving home from work each evening after dinner then watching TV a new experience we waited until a program was telecast. There was nothing telecast during the day. If you had your TV on during daytime you just received a test pattern. Finally the evening news was broadcast and some programs began.. At this time Roller Derby was big and we enjoyed it. Friday Night Fights were a big attraction to and finally a show called the Texaco Star Theater with Milton Berle.

Being I was attending Electric School under the G I bill of rights and receiving $ 95 a month and this was my only income. I attended school 8 AM until 12 noon daily. Our rent was calculated at $22.50 a month. This included all utilities. If you were able to get a phone, you paid that yourself. Phones were at a premium to there was a shortage. I was offered a job at Bufano's Service Station from 2pm until 6pm Monday through Friday servicing cars and 8hrs on Saturday doing lubrications. We always had money in our pocket.

OUR DAUGHTER JESSICA'S BIRTH

NINETEEN MONTHS AFTER AL'S BIRTH. In Aug 29,1948 our daughter Jessica was born on 8/29/1948 and we later moved to a 2 bedroom Apt on the second floor at 303 Gartside Ct with Lillian's mother Edna Johnson. My father visited us quite often and one time our son Al was admitted to the Chester Hospital with whopping cough. In the hospital they had him in a tent, when my father went to visit him he stood up and collapsed the tent when he saw his grandfather. My father E Charles visited us quite often. He was very fond of his grandchildren. After a year in Electrical School in Philadelphia was completed in 1948 I was looking for employment in the electrical field. My father E Charles happened to get a lead about a contractor looking for help.

MY APPRENTISHIP WITH CAMILLO CASCIATO

I WAS LATER WAS ABLE to acquire an apprentice with an electrical contractor named Camillo Casciato (Kelly) for nickname In Woodlyn Pa in 1948. this new position as an electrical apprentice tuned out very good. I was able to receive all types of training. Kelly took all kinds of electrical work. Residential, commercial and industrial. I really had the opportunity to gain a good experience with Kelly. We were a little cramp at 303 Garside court and my father & Grandfather's home in Norwood would become vacant and in about 1951 We moved from 303 Gartside Ct to their home at 113 Garfield Ave Norwood. This was one of the longest moves of my life. Moving my belongings in a panel truck. The trip from Chester to Norwood was quite a distance. My boss gave me a day to move and loaned me his truck to use. I was grateful when this move was finished. After I completed my apprentice training and was making $1.80 an hour. After being employed 5 yrs in 1953 I left this position. and took a position with Sun Oil Co.

SUN OIL CO and SON MICHAEL'S BIRTH

MY WIFE LILLIAN WAS IN Chester Hospital a week prior to her giving birth. On June 6 1953 my son Michael was born I was employed at the Sun Oil Co as a second class electrician at $2.48 an hour and was promoted to 1st class electrician at $2.82 an hour, this was a big increase in wages a dollar more than I made previous, but this job only lasted 5 months, job was completed and I was laid off with the intention of being hired back the following year. Sun Oil Co decided to no longer do their own construction. but To contract it out. This left me thinking on what could I do next. The state uemployment called me about a position with an electrical contractor I took an electrical position with another Contractor named Wight's Service doing residential and commercial work and this one lasted about a year in 1954 I was laid off and he referred me to another contractor wiring new constructed home and this job lasted about 3 months in 1955.I read the daily paper and found a job with a small contractor but his work was small and I wasn't getting 40hrs. Employment as an Electrician was hard to find at this time until I came across this add

DUPONT CO HIRING ELECTRICIANS

IN THE DAILY TIMES FOR electricians at the Dupont Co. I motored down to Pennsgrove NJ and applied for this job. I was hired and this process lasted several days compared to other employers. I was employed by the DuPont Co at Pennsgrove NJ on a construction job. I and other employees created a car pool and we met at the Chester Bridgeport Ferry daily and one of us drove his car for that week to the Dupont Co in Pennsville NJ.This ferry crossing was nice until about October when one morning the weather became very foggy. We could hear the fog horns from the approaching ferry and our ferry getting close and closer. Then out into the clear they both appeared to collide, head on. both used right rudder to pass each other. Well our Ferry missed his port and almost went aground, fortunately it was put in reverse and avoided this. We finally were able to get across safely. This construction job at DuPont's was getting to it end and in November 1955 it finally ended. While living in Norwood at 113w Garfield Ave quite amount of yard work was required mowing grass and trimming hedges and raking leaves. While living there I enrolled in a home electronic course. I made a work bench in the basement and done my studying there. One morning in early October I arose and the house was little chilly I set the thermostat up and was in our kitchen eating breakfast before leaving for work. I heard this big noise from the basement I investigated and found our heating boiler had broken. and water was pouring out. Later that day I contacted my father E Charles and my brother Harry who was in the heating business and he ordered a new heating boiler from Chester Supply. After he and I spent several evenings and a weekend a new heater was finally installed. My brother commented on my installation and piping saying how nice it was. After an oil tank was installed and filled, Harry checked the burner and started it. Everything came out ok.

OUR 4TH CHILD WAS BORN

OUR 4TH CHILD A SON we named Walter was born May 1 1956. Walter weighed 13lbs 3oz a heavy weight. Walter was kept for another week in Chester Hospital before being discharged. My brother Harry and his family while living at the Overlook housing and were looking for new

quarters and read this add for new housing sales in the daily papers of a development called Marshall Terrace Homes in Linwood Pa. He related this to me. My wife Lillian and I went down to Tour the sample home and found out that no down payment was required just a $100 good faith deposit that was returned at settlement. We applied for a home on Fronfield ave and were accepted. About a week later another section was now open and we selected an end house numbered 120 Ervin Ave. We made settlement for a mortgage of $10,200 and moved into 120 Ervin Ave on about October 2 1956. We hade new storm windows and storm doors installed prior to moving in. We were about the first family to move in on Ervin Ave at this date. Our first evening while sitting in our living room we received a welcome from someone in the old adjacent neighborhood a big stone came crashing through our new front storm door. I opened the front door and saw no one.

COLORADO FUEL & IRON later called PHOENIX STEEL CORP

I FOUND EMPLOYMENT IN NOVEMBER1955 at The Colorado Fuel & Iron Co hired as an electrician. They were building an additional building of 1000 ft to do fabricating. It was a cold winter on this job. I worked there doing electrical construction. I was asked to take a maintenance job as a motor inspector with the same rate of pay in a shop called the flange shop were heads of all sizes were flanged into shape or press out in the new press shop. Many propane heads 37 in in diameter were made. I was laid off in1960 after the plant was bought by The Phoenix Steel Corp and I was hired back 9 months later. During this time I found a job through the employment office at the Reynolds Spring Works in Chester Pa. The day that I was hired a fellow worker said to me that production has fallen, well 4 weeks later I was let go. A short time later Reynolds Spring moved their facility to Michigan. On my return to The Phoenix Steel Corp The new owners decided to renovate the plant with a new rolling mill, new shears and layout floor. On the steel production side were, 2 new electric furnaces and a continuous casting machine. Shutting down the Open Hearth Furnaces. During the construction of the new Melting Shop I was sent there to observe and learn about the new equipment being installed. I was present when the first Electric Furnace went into operation in September 1968. After about a year I was assigned as a temporary Electrical Forman. I held this position when to fill in when other foremen were on vacation. I bid on a job

Alfred Spevak

that I once held as an electrician in construction which did many new installations of all kinds. I enjoyed working with this group. It was all day work and the jobs were more interesting. At times I filled in as Foreman here to.

OUR LAST CHILD

ON JUNE 30 1959 MY son Jeffrey was born in Chester Hospital. As my family grew, my need for more income grew. I became a moonlighter doing all kinds of electrical and carpenter work. I took on electrical work and many construction jobs to increase my household income. I installed many kitchens abt 12 and bathrooms and other rooms. My work became professional looking, doing ceramic and vinyl tile. Carpenter work. Working with Laminates building counter tops, hanging doors, doing plumbing and of course electrical too. I did large installations of complete electrical at the new Minutella's Flower show room at 5th and Concord Ave in Chester Pa also the original Bufano's care wash at Providence Ave in Chester Pa

ONE DREADFUL PHONE CALL THE DEATH OF BETSEY WELCH

ONE SATURDAY NIGHT OF JANUARY 1962 My wife Lillian and I were getting ready to retire when our phone rang at this late hour. Lillian's mother Edna being close by answered. The call was from the Phildelphia morgue looking for relatives of a Betsy White who is Lillian's sister. Edna dropped the phone and called for her daughter Lillian. Lillian completed the call and arrangements were made for us to be at the morgue on Sunday at noon. Lillian and her brother Walter his spouse Margaret and I traveled to the Philadelphia morgue. Lillian and Walter were both were questioned for information about their sister Betsy. It came time to view the body and Walter and I were the only ones allowed. Betsy was on a slab and appeared blue looking. The four of us left and went to Betsy's Apartment looking for things of value and some insurance policy. We didn't find any but we later heard that she worked a a restaurant as a cashier and was insured for $1500. We left her apartment to make arrangement at the John Clancy funeral home. We left all the arrangement to the director to be as low as possible, it was $750. He sent a hearse to Philadelphia to claim the body. They didn't release the body until further tests were taken. The body was finaly released the following day and her body was frozen. She was laid out for viewing and I thought she looked like another person. The director said when he received the body she a frozen stiff. There was no more than 6 of us to see her buried. Betsy left an automobile a 1939 oldsmobile convertible under a fictitious name Betsy White. This may have been her modeling name. It was finally determined

128

the car did belong to Betsy. My father E Charles helped us getting the title. Walter kept after the coroner for a death certificate to no avail. I suppose they were still investigating her death. We did later find out that a male person had contacts with her and he was under surveillance by the narcotic squad At Betsy's death her apartment was searched. After many days a certificate of death was finally issued and the cause of death was suicide The $1500 insurance was not paid. We were able to sell the automobile to satisfy funeral expenses. Did Betsey commit suicide? To this day there was no real proof that she did. We did find out that she had some guests in the night before her death. When her girl friends called and received no answer, they did enter her apartment saw her stretched across the bed looked as if her reaching for the phone. For quite some time after her death we did received calls looking for Betsy. Born in 1927 died in 1962 at a young age of 34 years.

MY SON ALFRED BEING DRAFTED INTO THE MILITARY

MY SON AL GRADUATED FROM St James High School in 1965. He was able to get employment at the Reynolds Spring Co in Chester Pa. He worked there about a year and he received his military draft notice. I didn't want my son Al to be drafted and sent to Vietnam. I tried to get him to join the Navy where I thought he would be safer. He didn't want the longer enlistment. I was present when he left Media Pa for military service. I didn't want him to be drafted into the Army. Everyone drafted at the time of the Vietnam War saw service there. While stationed in Vietnam he sent us these 3in audible tapes. I went out and purchased a player for the tapes he sent us. It was nice hearing his voice. We carried his tapes and played them for all relatives that we visited.. Our family couldn't waited for the 2 years to pass by for his return home. He flew straight home to the Philadelphia Airport where we met him. This was a big relief for all of us for his safe return. He wasn't given any treatment before his discharge. After returning home he just sat around doing nothing but eat. He became overweight before he was able settle down to normalcy. He later was able to receive employment at the Philadelphia Electric & Gas Co. As my children grew and left home I had some money and I started to do woodworking. I purchased a Shop Smith 5 in one tool. I started with small projects and found that I was able to build some furniture projects. I subscribed for a magazine called Woodworkers Journal in it was plans to build a grandfather clock. After completing the clock I than built a cradle and 4 additional clocks for my children and some 4 drawer chests, Desk clocks, stools and lazy susans etc.. This was one of the nicest times of my life. I was relaxed my children were grown. I didn't need to look for much needed income to support the family. They were grown and on their own. I enjoyed woodworking, making all kinds of projects.

POMPANO BEACH 1986

MY SISTER BERTHA AND HUSBAND Franklin had this 2 weeks
of time sharing at Pompano Beach In Florida. Bertha invited me and
my wife Lillian down to spend time with them. I was finally able to
make plans for the invitation. I told her that I would have to schedule
a vacation time from work during the preceding year. We finally got
together for this to happen. In the later part of February1986 my wife
Lillian and I flew down to Fort Lauderdale Florida where my sister
Bertha and her husband Franklin met us and drove use to there time
share apartment at Pompano beach FL for a 2 week stay. Just about
every evening the four of us sat down to play pinochle. During the
2nd week cousin Jack and wife Nora arrived from their new home at
Barefoot Bay where they had just moved to in September 1985. Jack
and wife Nora had previously lived in Ft Lauderdale FL We all had
a great time there. Frank and Jack taking a day playing golf. One
night we attended a stage show where Mickey Rooney and Ann Miller
performed. Another night we went for cocktails to a rotating bar atop
of a building called Pier 66. This turned out to be on of the most
enjoyable trips that my wife Lillian and I had during our lives. The
first time for her to travel a great distance by air. She said she would
never fly. She did and enjoyed the flight.

RETIREMENT

I FINALLY RETIRED AFTER 30 yrs employment at the Phoenix Steel Corp December 31 1986 at 64 years of age. I received my first Social Security Check on February 3 1987. I was still making wood projects in my cellar

MY SADDIST MOMENT IN MY LIFE

MY WIFE AND I WERE getting along fairly well. Then one night in December 22 1989 my wife arrived home from her friend Roses home and didn't feel well and she told me to call her close friend Rose. Rose came and decided to call our family doctor and was told to call 911.Paramedics arrived and checked her out and gave her treatment before transporting her to Sacred Heart Hospital. Rose went along in the ambulance and I followed in my car. While I was signing my wife up for Hospital admittance, Rose came towards me and said it doesn't look very good, the doctors are using the paddles on her chest. We waited and finally one of the Nuns came up to Rose and I and talked to us and without giving any information, we were taken to another room and given the news of her death. After both of us broke down and some time later I was able to call my family. When they arrived after she was cleaned up we were able to view her. Funeral Service was conducted at Wards Funeral Home in Linwood Pa with a Funeral Mass at Holy Saviour Church with burial at Lawn Croft Cemetery. Luncheon at Holy Saviour Hall.

AFTER LILLIAN'S PASSING

AFTER THE DEATH OF MY wife I went to Florida with my brother-in-law Franklin Embon and it was strange because 3yrs previous in 1986 there were 4 of us at Pompano Beach Fl. My sister Bertha had passed on near her birth date in 1987.We stopped at Barefoot Bay and visited with Jack and Nora Teuchert. Stayed there for about a week traveling with Jack and a group of seniors entertaining seniors. Frank and I traveled down to the time share at Pompano Beach and met with his sons Allan and Kevin and their friends. After 2 weeks we traveled back to Jack and Nora's home for another week. Franklin and I left Jack & Nora and traveled across Florida to Port Richey Fl to visit the Sheeky brothers James and William. I worked with James Sheeky at Phoenix Steel and Franklin worked at Sun Oil with William Sheeky. We stayed there overnight. Sunday Morning James took me to this most beautiful Catholic Church for mass. The church was a round building with a slopping floor and stained glass window. The remaining part of the day James drove us around for site seeing. We finally left for home. After being away for about 4 weeks, upon arriving at home my daughter presented me with a large box of mail for me to sort.

WHAT SHOULD I DO NOW

WELL EVERYONE HAS A JOB for me. I ended up doing a job for my son Michael and wife Patricia at there place in Selbyville De. The first job was to build a 10 by 12 shed for storage. After completing this we started converting the attached garage for an addition to the living room. I was there several weeks going back home on Fridays and returning on Mondays. What's next Well My Son Walt had job to do. I complete a renovation After building a 12 x 16 dining room addition and new kitchen in 1988 My wife Lillian, Franklin Embon, Kevin, Jessica, Woody had Thanksgiving dinner there. Walt and wife Maureen decided to replace all windows complete, new siding drywall stairway and new dormers. This job took a lot of time and help it looks good with the new brick front. I thought my job was complete until later my son Mike and I put in a new tub in the bathroom.

PARTNERSHIP

ON OF MY LATE WIFE'S friends Rose Zalewski's sister Gloria May's husband George died and was looking for a place to stay. Rose asked me and after much thought It was decided Gloria would cook all of my meals and split a expenses 50-50. This worked out very well for both of us. Gloria's and my children and grandchildren visited us frequently. We had many great events visiting her daughter in Cape May and them coming to Linwood. This lasted about 5yrs and I decided to sell my home in late1997 and move in with my daughyer Jessica. Gloria moved to an apartment next to her sister in Eddystone Pa and I moved in with my daughter Jessica with son-in-law Elwood (woody) Adams and have been here quite some time. While visiting my Niece Sandy and Nephew Paul Rucker, I was in a conversation with cousin John Teuchert and Franklin Embon discussing computers. I didn't have one and decided to buy a computer and this happened to be one of best things that I accomplished during my life. After receiving the computer and learning how to operate it, I wa able to do many operations.

AN ADDENDUM OF EVENTS

I REMEMBER IN 1927 WHEN I was 4 1/2 years old our family was getting ready to attend the 100 anniversary of the Baltimore & Ohio RR now named CSX in Baltimore MD. We left by train from the B&O station at Fairview Road in Woodlyn Pa. I remember sitting in stands at this event and viewing the first locomotive on rails in motion. just a short time ago I saw this same locomotive on video tape during the Rail Fair of 1997. It was great to be at this anniversary.

MY FIRST TIME IN OCEAN CITY NJ

THE NEIGHBORS THAT LIVED CLOSE by named Welsh had relatives that owned a small rooming house in Ocean City NJ. I was about 9 yrs old at this time and my father took me down to this place for a weekend stay. This building was very old. Probably built in the 1800's. It had wainscoting about 4ft high on all of the walls, floors were bare wood. Our room on the second floor we slept in a painted white iron bed with a bureau close by where a large pottery bowl placed upon it and with an enormous pottery pitcher for water for washing standing on the floor nearby There was a bathroom at the end of the hall for all roomers. The 1st and main floor contained a large table for dinning family style. It appeared as I look back that this place was close to the ocean. I remember bathing that day the water was warm enough. I felt a little uncomfortable spending time in this rooming house. It was strange to me at that time.

BETHLEHEM STEEL CO

IN 1935 I WAS 12YRS old then my father E Charles Spevak was ordered by the Baldwin Locomotive Works where he was employed to go to the Bethlehem Steel Company in Bethlehem, Pa. His job was to dismantle some patterns for shipment back to the Baldwin plant. These patterns were for the hydro turbines of Hoover Dam and the The Baldwin Locomotive Co was required to store these for several years. We arrived in Bethlehem and stayed at the Bethlehem Hotel for 2 nights. The first day I went along with my father to the Bethlehem Steel office and remember crossing the street to a restaurant where tables were set for workers of the steel plant. I believe at that time a worker could receive a good lunch for 35 cents. The following day my father had to enter the plant and I had to stay put. Before leaving the hotel Dad handed me a five dollar bill from his expense money for me to get breakfast and lunch. That 5 dollars was a lot of money back then. I decided to take a walk. Well I walked a great many miles and I may have circled the plant. I stopped at a small eatery and had lunch. The following day my Dad's job was finished and other than returning home he decided for us to take a trip to Brooklyn NY to visit friends or relatives.

OUR TRIP TO BROOKLYN NY

I REMEMBER THE TRIP IN his 1933 4 door Plymouth sdn and the drive through the Holland Tunnel and after arriving in Brooklyn NY my dad asked a policeman for direction to this particular address. The police directed my father to an Alderman's office and we found that we were only I street away. The family that we visited I didn't know their names. The husband was the in charge of the apartments. He was called the Apt super. I don't know who these people were to this day. We stayed there overnight and the following day we traveled out on the Island to a town called Franklin Square a suburban are where their son lived and had a business constructing bank metal partitions etc, in his garage. We were there for a short visit before leaving for the long trip home.

RINGLING BROS, BARNUM & BAILEY CIRCUS

ABOUT 1933 MY FATHER HAD taken me for a trip to Erie Avenue in Philadelphia to see the circus under the famous big top which they were still using at that time. This was enormous and left a big impression on me. I remember asking my father (how did they put this big tent up?) he said they used the elephants for their power of lifting. Of course the show was great. My Pop bought tickets for an additional Wild West Show that we saw too. I had a great day.

As I remember another time before my 10th birthday my cousin Frank and Jack Teuchert and I were taken by their grandfather Charles Geraghty by public transportation to 69st in upper Darby to see a circus. It was a small circus not Ringling bros but we did have a good day eating, I remember the cotton candy etc.

MILMONT PARK POST OFFICE

IN THE 1930'S MAIL WAS mostly transported by rail. Trains and street cars. I remember at train stations, seeing mail bags hanging close to the rails. As trains pass by the postal car would grab the mail bag without stopping. Most trains had a baggage car and a U S Postal car where mail was sorted and bagged for delivery. The postal dept was delivering mail at this time by Air called Air Mail faster delivery. Air mail required an additional postage, an air mail stamp. These were beautiful and some were collectable. I remember after WW2 an air mail bag was hung between to upright poles and was picked up at the Buckman Airport this lasted for a short time.

THE OUTINGS AT RIVEVIEW BEACH NEW JERSEY

AS I REMEMBER MY FIRST trip to Riverview Beach. it was quite an experience. It was the mode of travel how we arrived there. Back in the 1920's and 30's travel was mostly by street car or train. Well Riverview Beach located in southern part of New Jersey along the Delaware River; we traveled to there by boat. I remember our family waiting at the Market street wharf in Chester Pa for the Wilson Line Boat to arrive from Philadelphia. For the trip to Riverview Beach. The Wilson Line also scheduled moonlight cruises on the Delaware River. At Riverview Beach there was a pool and many amusement rides and tables to eat your picnic lunch that just about everyone brought along. After a most enjoyable day the trip back to Chester Pa aboard the Wilson Line was another treat. Riverview Beach is no longer an amusement park; I saw that a person nearby in New Jersey bought the train that once was part of the amusements. This train is operating on his estate. What; I remember in my early years. Men and children parting their hair in the middle. Males wearing knickers. I remember after graduating 8th grade of school receiving my first pair of long trousers. When I was in my early teens I was driven to Chester Pa to a store called Murray's and was fitted for my first dress suit. It was a light blue gabardine it fit perfectly and I loved wearing it.

IMPROVING CONDITIONS IN MILMONT PARK PA

INSTALLING A SEWAGE SYSTEM IN our town and eliminating cesspools. Curbs and sidewalks. Paving Belmont Ave and using a steam powered roller. This was probably the last time this steam powered roller was used. When I was young during Christmas we visited everyone that we knew that had an unde layout r the tree train. Train displays were big during this time. The Williams family directly across from our home had a big display in their dining room. Doors were closed and it took a couple of weeks to do. Back then trees were trimmed after the children were in bed. During a visit the people would offer you some of their Christmas candy. Out would come this big 5lb box of chocolates. Being the depression year money was scarce and the candy wasn't a top grade.

CONCLUSION

WHAT HAVE I LEARNED IN my life time? I had a great life. After all of my education. military service, apprentice as an electrician, marriage and raising a family of five children. 11 grandchildren and 10 g-grandchildren It all comes back to family, relatives and friends. Without these You end up short. I wish anyone reading my Biography find it enlightening. to see how people lived previously. I have the Spevak Family Tree and Spevak Pictures. I can see all of the changes made in my lifetime. I have listings of all deceased relatives in findagrave.com, for you to see Click on to my name anywhere you see it posted in findagrave and this will send you to my page and click on to my virtual cemetery. You will have to get registered to do this at findagrave. I have recorded all of my father E Charles Spevak's 16mm films on a DVD disk any one without one let me know. Everyone should keep a daily record of events that are happening during their lifetime. A diary would do. As you get older you are always looking back wishing that you had accomplished this. Life on earth is short if keep putting things off the time is lost doing this. Wishing everyone the best in life

Al Spevak
Alfred509@gmail.com

The green 1933 Willys 2 1920's Stearns
Knight 3 The rte 71 & 76 Trolleys
4 Al's 1930 Ford Roadster 5 Al's 1937 Willys
Bottom the 1920's Teuchert Parlor

CPSIA information can be obtained
at www.ICGtesting.com
Printed in the USA
BVHW031748140620
581492BV00002B/3/J

9 781490 758930